The underlying reason linking the omnivorous majority and partisans to countless cruelties is there to see and know, but we can't see and know that such weighty influence is an eternal natural law, as we are tempted to believe.

Animals:
Why They Must Not Be Brutalized

By Eye Irritancy Tests & LD50 Tests & Vivisection

Whaling & Abattoirs & Sport Hunting
Fur Farms & Sport Fishing & Circuses
Religious Sacrifice & Bull Fights
Puppy Mills & Dissection

Pigeon Shoots & Factory Farms
Horse & Grey Hound Racing & Animal Acts
Seal Clubbing & Roadside Zoos
Dog & Cock Fights & Rodeos
Xenotransplantation
Cramped Confinement
Trapping

Or In Any Other Inhuman Way

J. B. Suconik

Nuark Publishing

For information contact: Nuark Publishing, Post
Office Box 228 Elmhurst, Il 60126-3604.
Manufactured in the United States of America by
BookMasters, Inc.
This book printed on acid free paper.

Publisher's Cataloging-in-Publication
(Provided by Quality Books, Inc.)

Suconik, J.B.
      Animals : why they must not be brutalized /
J.B. Suconik. -- 1st ed.
      p. cm.
      Includes bibliographical references and index.
      LCCN: 99-96271
      ISBN: 0-9675560-0-7

      1. Animal rights. 2. Animal welfare.
3. Animal rights movement.   1. Title.

HV4711. S83 2000   179' .3
                                               QB199-1950

To the Memory of My Mother, and Father-

and Ushie Farber too

Sections

Sections

Preface

Words defied the attempt to accurately express my feelings of respect, gratitude, admiration, and affection for the amorphous community that comprises the "animal liberation movement." But the limitations imposed by words did not completely hamper the effort to write in passionate opposition to humanities demonic tyranny of animals.

Although emotions were inextricably involved, they could not function to substitute for the insights and outlook that could be made credible only by verifiable facts, and logical validity. I believe the resultant force of truth constitutes the conclusion that neither wild nor domestic animals should not be randomly, or constantly brutalized in the alleged interest of human animals.

J. B. Suconik   Elmhurst, Illinois

Acknowledgements

When I approached Tina Birnbaum, Ingrid Niinemae, and Ileene F. Sedlacek and asked if they would become involved in this project, their immediate assent was a thing to remember.

The comments, and suggestions, of Mrs. Birnbaum and Mrs. Niinemae were details of enhancement that a serious effort should not dispense with.

Included in that description was the work of Ileene F. Sedlacek who received the manuscript on my allegedly converted floppy disk and created these pages from what can be best described as "mish mash." I will always be grateful to these people for these things to remember.

1

Opening Comments

Books of this genre, including this one, would not have been written if brutalizing animals were limited to ravenous creatures in "the wild" struggling to survive. Would it be realistic or unrealistic to assert that such hungry predators should not prey upon other animals? And, would it be absurd to say that neither wild, nor domestic animals should be subjected to the endless tyranny of human predators? "Unrealistic" must be this writers answer to the first question. As to the second query, the sole purpose of this book is to affirm that animals should not be subjected to the tyranny of humans. To cite the obvious, the unavoidable dictates of nature demand prudent resignation. The dictates of humans however, entails **preventable** wholesale and often frivolous brutality, and breeds passionate opposition by those I would characterize as a humane biocentric minority, to whom there can be no resignation to brutality.

The morbid human brutishness, visible and invisible, is without intermission, or end: the fiat of habituation, interest, custom, and belief in the divine right of human dominion over animals that degenerates in practice to the divine right of humans to tyrannize animals.

In a world of perpetual change, we ourselves are subject to change, along with our habits, customs, thoughts, and beliefs. Thus a belief held by a "rational" species that degenerates in practice to the right to tyrannize another species will, I believe, like that of the 17th' century belief in the divine right of kings, fade away and be relegated to the order of misinterpreted and mishandled beliefs.

To paraphrase a line from Shakespeare's "King Lear," I must stop thinking that such blind subservience to habit, interest, custom, ignorance, and misconception is not corrigible, "that way madness lies." That I have stopped thinking that way is made self-evident, I believe, in the following pages.

2

Inference and Speculation

*Could the young but realize how soon they will
become mere walking bundles of habit, they would give
more heed to their conduct while still in the plastic
state. We are spinning our own fates, good or evil,
and never to be undone.*

William James--Papers on Philosophy

There seems to be no shirking the conclusion, based on concrete evidence provided by bone-bearing sediment, and artifacts, that our primeval ancestors exploited animals. Can we infer that it probably facilitated survival and speculate that violent exploitation born of compelling need degenerated over time into a deadly habit? Poet John Dryden's trenchant insight provides a thought-provoking concept about the unlimited influence of habit.

*We first make our habits, and then our habits make us.
All habits gather by unseen degrees,
as brooks make rivers, rivers run to seas.*

Our civilization today is a sea, polluted by man as never before with the blood of billions upon billions of "only animals." Thus another book evolves, purporting to present

Inference and Speculation

justification for the emancipation of animals from human tyranny. The test by which such a claim must be judged must be coldly rational and objective. Do the facts invoked sustain the interpretations adduced? Are the premises well grounded? Do the conclusions based upon them follow with logical necessity, and sustain the justification as claimed?

At issue in the dispute between biocentric animal advocates and their anthropocentric opposition, is whether or not the animal kingdom should continue to be subjected to human exploitation which, inevitably entails human tyranny. Antianimal partisans maintain that animals are, in terms of human interest, expendable items. Included in this category is the divine right element insisting on man's right to exploit animals: methods and consequences notwithstanding. Thus, we are told:

> An animal does not have a soul, can't experience pain as we do, must eventually die, why not in man's behalf?

> Progress in human, and veterinary medicine depends to a great degree on unfettered experiments on animals.

> Many animals prey upon other animals, why should they not be preyed upon by humans?

> Shall it be your child, or Fido?

As we shall see, such rhetoric cannot survive thoughtful rebuttal, but is nevertheless, a contributing factor to the unceasing torment of animals. Unfortunately, most people are ignorant of the gruesome facts.

Inference and Speculation

Some examples of what we humans are doing to animals are mentioned in section thirteen; the whole story, not being known, can never be told. But that story would be, if we can speculate from what is known, a revolting record of cyclopedic dimensions.

That record is history, which we are powerless to change. The future, however, is not beyond our power to affect. If history is not to be a prophesy of the future, the present must be employed as an agent for change to a world not sullied by the injustice of human generated tyranny of animals. And let me not be told that this is a cry for equal rights for animals, which would be prima facie nonsense.

The rescue of animals from human tyranny in a comprehensive sense must ultimately entail a moral and legal transformation of heroic dimensions, predicated on reason and on an old but augmented principle of justice, as formulated in the next section. "Nature red in tooth and claw" is outside the human pale, and will stay in regard to predation as constituted. Those who find such realism depressing may find solace in my paraphrase of an ancient Roman aphorism: Beyond one's power, one is not obliged to act. Another extension of justice, however, is not beyond collective human power intent on no longer emulating "nature red in tooth and claw."

3

Justice and Power

Justice and power must be brought together,
so that whatever is just may be powerful,
and whatever is powerful may be just.
Blaise Pascal

We can infer from the school of experience that people have liked and loved animals since antediluvian times, and callously tyrannized them for incalculable aeons. Can the demise of such long lived terrorism in all of its brutal forms, become a reality in the foreseeable future? I believe that the above words of Pascal provide one of the necessary conditions of the passing of such brutality.

Justice and Power

That evasive goal will require the power of Partisan justice. By Partisan justice I mean as "supporter, backer, champion," as opposed to "biased, prejudiced, warped," which is one definition of the adjective partisan. Henceforth the noun Partisan defined as "supporter, backer, champion" will be capitalized; the adjective partisan defined as "biased, prejudiced, warped," will not be capitalized.

Having studied various readings about the requirements of justice, and having been painfully aware of the more than occasional disparity between requirements, and concrete realities, I have concluded that realities are often a woefully flawed distortion of justice. More particularly, that which passes for justice in the animal human context is an overwhelmingly partisan conception of justice, i.e., "biased, prejudiced, warped."

Justice in the abstract, broadly defined, consists in theory of each individual receiving what is his or her due, from which it follows that justice in principle is not divisible. But principle has proven to be no match for the influence of interest, legitimized by partisan justice, which has classified various races, nationalities, and ethnic groups as inferior, and which still classifies animals as exploitable property.

I believe that the principle of justice should be extended to the entire animal kingdom, which would repudiate the classification of animals as human property. An end to the commerce in living flesh, blood, and bones, and all the unspeakable fear and suffering that that entails, can occur only through the intervention of Partisans seeking that goal, without which, animals will continue to be tyrannized by humans, as they are today, and have been for aeons of yesterdays. To think otherwise is not realistic.

When two entities have been consistently causally connected, they probably will continue to be so in the future if nothing intervenes to sever the connection. Tyranny was causally connected with slavery in America as both a cause and effect. That connection was severed by internecine war. Can we believe that the tyranny suffered by animals can be terminated without an enormous, but bloodless conflict between partisans for the status quo, and Partisans for justice? At stake are the degenerate offspring of partisans for the status quo a non exhaustive account would include:

Factory farms	Branding	Abattoirs
Sport fishing	Captive whales	Starving
Ld50 test	Trapping	Fur farms
Vivisection	Religious sacrifice	Freezing
Bullfighting	Cock fighting	Crushing
Animal acts	Sport hunting	Isolation
Burning	Pigeon shoots	Dog fights
Electrocuting	Puppy Mills	Whaling
Premarin Mares	Infecting	Rodeo brutality
Roadside zoos	Seal clubbing	Horse soring
Mother/young separation		Draize Test
Castration without anesthetizing		

A pertinent but incomplete answer as to how such abominations came to be acceptable can be found in past and prevailing conceptions of justice. Implicit in one imposing symbol a blindfolded women a balance in one hand a sword in the other is the notion of justice, i.e., impartiality, fairness, giving each his or her due, and making right of wrong, and what is meant by "each" is a human being. "Justice," wrote Justinian, "is the constant desire and effort to render to every man his due." To Aristotle, "justice is to give every man his own." Cicero believed that "justice consists in doing no injury to men, decency in giving them no offense." "Justice," said John Stuart Mill, "is a name for certain classes of moral rules, which concern the essentials of human well-being more

Justice and Power

clearly, and are therefore of more absolute obligation than any other rules." According to Bertrand Russell, "only justice can give security: and by justice I mean the recognition of the equal claims of all human beings." We can be critical of such seemingly idealistic, but anthropocentric moral judgements, because they are also exclusionary sins of omission, reflecting perhaps an attitudinal continuum, concomitant with human existence.

The affliction of partisan exclusion of mice, cats, dogs, or other sentient creatures from the sphere of justice (to cite the obvious) has not infected everyone. The Jain community an outgrowth of dissent from Hinduism that is at least as old as Buddhism, has remained immune. Justice to a Jain entails, in principle, the right of all sentient life to be free of human tyranny. My letter to Uttam K. Jain, a luminary of the Chicago Jain community in which I requested relevant statistics, evoked the following (unedited) reply.

February 23, 1994

Dear Jack: It was a pleasure hearing from you. Regarding the violent crimes in Jain community, I do not have any statistics. However there have been crimes committed against the members of Community but not the other way around. There may have been some stray incidents of crimes committed by a member of the Jain Community. As a matter of fact I have heard of one incident that took place in a very small town in India where a husband knifed his wife and then cut her dead body into small pieces. In another one a lady was murdered and then thrown into a well. This crime was committed with the collaboration among the victim's husband and his parents. Above are the only incidents that I am aware of. However, I would look further into it to see if I could get some statistics, if available, by contacting some people in the Jain community. I wanted to get this letter out to you as a quick response to yours.

10

Justice and Power

The principle of Jainism, as you know, have a great impact on the behavior of the community as a whole and individuals as part of the community. My aversion towards the violence, especially the violence against the 'animals' has its strength derived from having been brought up in Jain environment. If I weren't born in Jain environment and brought up in it I might not have been so compassionate towards animals. Jainism is a way of life rather than just a religion for many Jains. The non violence is preached not for the sake of propagating Jainism but as a normal way of life, where violence is rejected because it is wrong and cruel. Jainism preaches compassion even towards those who cause harm to others. Out of all the wars this world has seen, none was started by a vegetarian community.

With regards Uttam

In the absence of experience, we can only speculate as to the realities of a world embracing the humane aspects of Jainism. However, the realities of a world in which partisan justice is pandemic comprises an inferno of malevolence, war, crime, and cruelty to which we are habituated, but the pronoun "we," does not imply everyone. The many Partisans who are not members of the Jain community vehemently oppose all forms of cruelty, and reject an aristocratic concept of justice that mercilessly terminates at the threshold of the animal kingdom.

But "change," as Ronald Glossop professor of philosophy at Edwardsville Illinois said, "is an everlasting reality." Telling evidence indicates that "We the people" are becoming less tolerant of the routine tyranny of animals. "We the people," that love our "pets" and hamburgers!

It is from this matrix of the absurd that Partisans for animals-legions of Partisans-must emerge, because adequate power and unflagging effort is the necessary condition of the ascendance of Partisan justice.

Justice and Power

There can be no denying the difficulties encountered
in trying to be just, or as noted above, the disparity between
justice in the abstract and concrete realities, or the paucity of
justice in relation to need and demand. But such facts have
failed to place a moratorium on either the quest, or realization of what was and is perceived as justice, and such facts
do not militate against the ultimate universal realization of
Partisan Justice. Global Partisan justice would ensure by law
that the most savage and protracted abuse of power could no
longer be tolerated, and as with all statutory rules of conduct, be subject to sanctions, as determined by law.

An idealistic outlook? Yes, and it can't be discredited
by a strong dose of realism. But no illusions should be em-
braced entailing the **universal** attainment of this social ideal
in the near future. In the absence of a monolithic human condition, and the diversity that that entails, there must be accommodation to ageless realities if the world is to eventually
achieve what cannot be accomplished at once. One of various situations demanding accommodation is subsistence hunting and fishing by indigenous cultures. It would be absurd,
and downright immoral, to expect Eskimoan people to starve
in the name of an alien Partisan justice.

At the time of this writing, no less than the time when
many Americans opposed the freeing of slaves, many Americans oppose the threat to their entrenched slaughterhouse
ethos. It may be therefore argued that the concept of Partisan
justice is utopian because one's pet or herd of cattle is considered to be one's property in a context of inviolable property rights. I would have to disagree. It doesn't follow from
the fact that millions of animals are classified as human property, that the concept of Partisan justice is utopian. How we
classify depends, by and large, upon our purpose. Slaves in
the antebellum south were classified as property because they

Justice and Power

could then be bought, sold, and exploited with impunity, and it is for the same reason that animals were classified as mere property. That that classification is still a reality may be attributable to widespread ignorance of its implications. To classify living flesh, blood, and bones as mere property, whether human or animal, is to condemn sentient life to real world hell, and that is what Mr. Homo Sapiens has been up to, but not without misgivings.

Exhibiting aversion toward the injustice, and tribal custom of their time, the framers of the U.S. Constitution excluded the word slavery, because as James Madison observed, "they did not choose to admit the right of property in man." They were influenced no doubt by the astute English philosopher, John Locke. Locke invented the expression liberation, which inspired and influenced the architects of the American Revolution, Declaration of Independence, and U.S. Constitution. It was Locke who perceived and postulated that "every man has a property in his own person; this nobody has a right to but himself." Was Locke's thesis valid?

If a man's home is his inviolate castle, can his own person be less inviolate? My hands that are typing this text are a part of my arms that are part of my body that constitute a person that is formulating concepts. The overarching interest that I share with others is life itself, which is a necessary condition of everything else. Thus I hold myself, as I should, and do hold others, to be an inviolate organism, not to be banished to the sphere of property, or brutally exploited, or unjustly incarcerated, or deprived of life except under exceptional circumstances such as a capital violation, as stipulated by the statutory laws of society. Laws are formulated to maintain order, protect life, and punish vice: or more specifically, to selectively punish vice.

The cat that I shared my home with, and cared for, did

not indignantly say "you stepped on my tail" when I inadvertently did so, but with a shattering yowl conveyed that message. To say that the cat's tail is not the cat's tail and property, would be as absurd and fallacious as saying that everything that constitutes the cat is not the cat's property. The word property derives from the Latin *proprietas*, the noun form of the Latin *proprius,* meaning one's own. Everything that constitutes the cat is the cat's own property. By extension, every sentient creature has a property in itself which should, if we are to abide by our own principle of justice, prohibit human ownership and brutal exploitation of animals as it prohibits ownership and exploitation of humans.

It could be objected that my thesis is mistaken, because of the many animals enjoying a good life as human property. We need to substitute the word slaves for the word animals, to perceive how silly that rebuttal would be. That many slaves had kind masters, did not justify slavery and its unspeakable cruelties. And the fact that many animals have kind masters and good homes, can't justify the classification of animals as human property and its unspeakable cruelties. However kind masters and good homes are a good portent for a new just world for animals.

By one definition, to liberate is "to set free, as from oppression, confinement, or from foreign control." It seems, then, that a necessary condition of liberation as defined, will be the demise of the animal as human property enterprise, which will be, regrettably, a slow death.

Persistent and prudent Partisan effort has engendered various reforms, and must continue to do so, because such effort and success are the step by step preliminaries to the demise of mankinds most egregious custom. Reforms notwithstanding, there are on this inhumane day, as there was yesterday, and will be tomorrow, millions of doomed animal

Justice and Power

on humanity's death rows for its living animal property.

Such is the reality behind a facade of benign religiosity and sophisticated modernity, in a world in which John Van Brugh believed that "custom is the law of fools." Custom is not everyone's authoritarian boss. There are other masters, such as the internal world of feeling and reflection, without which we would not be what we are, and would not be moved to non-violent action. Thus there will not be another Gettysburg on behalf of animals.

Returning to the charge of utopianism. That critique would indicate, I believe, antipathy to the notion of Partisan justice, and one's purpose, to depreciate the concept. We can be certain that a world in which utopianism was nonexistent, would be in a negative sense, other than what it is.

The inveterate realist perceives the realities of yesterday and today, as harbingers of tomorrow. The inveterate utopian tends to ignore such realities, enthralled as it were with what is desired for tomorrow. Theoretically, primordial forms of life that first ventured from the brine to dry land were rudimentary utopians.

Can we conceive of a better brief for utopianism? Whether one is willing to acknowledge it or not, many utopian dreams of the past are today's realities. The possibility of flying from one antipode to another in a machine, or humans walking on the moon, or the abolition of slavery in America was at one time the stuff of utopian dreams.

But one half of the story will not do. The other half is that dreams without means are of no practical significance. And means are obscure. Not knowing how to reach an insensitive, uninformed, and misinformed public, Partisans try out various tactics, hoping to learn from experience. They support hundreds of organizations, demonstrate, write letters, lobby politicians, write books, and disseminate literature.

Justice and Power

Many open their homes to stray, sick, and hungry animals, and establish shelters, and sanctuaries without which, many animals would pitiably perish. To cite the not so obvious, we are here in the presence of de facto Partisan justice, the precurser of de jure Partisan justice.

The tactics employed to achieve a de jure system of justice must be predicated, I believe, on a variation of Locke's principle of justice: i.e., every sentient creature has a property in itself; this nobody has a right to in the human context of inviolable property rights. Such tactics must entail unflagging effort in pursuit of the objective: Defenders of the predatory way of life, allegedly formed in the infancy of mankind, will not yield to the logic of reason and justice without a protracted struggle to maintain a fierce and cruel status quo.

And how, one might prudently ask, does a biocentric minority prevail against an omnivorous, uninformed majority? Prevailing, as history affirms, has previously occurred by small forces over larger ones, by virtue of a factor described in Tolstoy's "War and Peace," Part XIV, Chapter 11. For Tolstoy the force of an army is a function of the rank and file, enhanced by an ineffable something, best described as the spirit of the army. It was Tolstoy's purpose to emphasize the fact, affirmed by experience, that numerical superiority is not necessarily the decisive factor in conflicts between opposing camps.

It was an ineffable something fostering the efforts of Partisans that engendered reforms in the past, as I aver it will in the future. The ineffable something can be described not as spirit, but as an emotional turbulence produced by empathy, anger, compassion, outrage, and a sense of justice defiled.

A partisan verbal attack may attempt to condemn the analogy between animals and people as false. Animals, as we know from the many tragic results of vivisection, are not perfect biological and psychological analogs for humans. Every analogy must (AT SOME POINT,) break down. But that truism was and is not a deterrent for the vivisection enterprise.

Since antiquity, animals were thought to be biologically analogous with humans, resulting in their unconscionable, and often frivolous use as experimental subjects. A world that has literally tortured and killed untold millions of creatures in the name of analogy can't rationally deny its rationale to avoid the humane consequences of its classification of animals as human analogs. I must labor the point because facts must not be perceived as ambiguities. A valid analogy entails significant similarities between different things, and can be an important factor in reasoning, if the quantity of shared qualities is adequate. In addition to the biological similarities between humans and animals there are shared psychological qualities. A careful reading of Masson's and Mc Carthy's "When Elephants Weep" allows the reader to discover germane realities. Their book is a scientific and field-note account of the animal world, in which emotions such as joy, compassion, depression, happiness, fear, rage, and even an esthetic sense, are manifest. What we might characterize as animal history is replete with examples of animals risking their lives to save their own kind, as well as humans. The 1997 Britannica Book of the Year page 214, tells the story of Binta Jua, an eight-year-old gorilla, and her display of concern on behalf of a human child. She picked up the three year old boy that had fallen into her enclosure, and placed him at the door where he could be retrieved by his own kind. We can deduce from such behavior a desire to facilitate the removal of the helpless child. And who can say with certitude that this wild and powerful animal did not reveal concern for the well being of the child?

My unscientific opinion, based on a lifetime of casual observation, is that animals communicate not only with humans, but with one other in their own animal manner. Impressed as we are with our alleged divine right to exploit them (and the power to do so), we have not found it significant that we don't have a monopoly on the ability to communicate, or build shelters, or make and use tools, or experience pain and suffer. And we forget that it was according to one school, the same evolutionary phenomenon that spawned both mice and men with similar physiological attributes. The issue is not whether or not an analogy based on telling evidence is *valid*. Our unsympathetic, immoral use of animals as human analogs in the revolting vivisection enterprise has foreclosed that question, for nothing, by authority of a law of contradiction can both **be and not be**. Thus an animal can not be, and not be a human analog.

"Change" which "is an everlasting reality," has not spared the belief that some people could be morally and legally classified as mere property. At one brutish time a hypothetical Mr. Jones' foot and everything else comprising Jones could be the legal property of a hypothetical Mr. Smith, philosophers, statesmen, and morality notwithstanding. Change precipitated by war intervened, and the whole of Jones the slave became inviolable property not accessible to Smith or anyone else.

Thus it follows by valid analogy as described above: A)The faulty classification of animals (and humans)as property, predicated on interest, custom, and ignorance, was a deplorable tragic decision. B) Everything that constitutes an animal is the animals inviolable property, and cannot morally be the property of people living in a normative arrangement of inviolable property rights. The animal as property concept

18

Justice and Power

should succumb, as the human as property concept has, to the requirements of rightful change. Property and life are of different and discordant spheres. The sphere of property to which we have condemned animals as we once condemned humans is the sphere of legal possession. The sphere of life is a nanosecond between eternities, which we know from tragic heartbreaking experience, can not be entrusted to the former. A murderous war will not intervene for the animals, but justice and Partisan power can.

4

Necessity

And with necessity, the tyrant's plea, excused his devilish deeds.
                                                        John Milton

And with necessity, the vivisectors plea attempts to justify their tyranny. Obscured is the fact that vivisection, like a game of chance, occurs in the sphere of contingent events where nothing happens of necessity. At various times in the past the concept of "necessity" was used to justify torture, witch burning, human sacrifice, concentration camps, cannibalism. And it is the word "necessity" as a rationale for vivisection and its many horrid implications that must be elucidated.

An indifferent or unreflective mind can be led astray, and influenced by the testimony of "authority," which is not to imply that the testimony of "authority," may not be, and is not often a factor of great value. It is the partisan testimony of "authority," whether predicated on interest, or lack of careful deliberation, that can often be misleading.

Readers of the Food and Drug Administration's "Consumer," February 1989, were notified that: "Research on laboratory animals will continue to be necessary in the foreseeable future." According to a committee of the National Research Council, the Foundation for Biomedical Research declared: "There is a compelling reason for using animals in research. The reason is that we have no other choice. Virtually all medical knowledge and treatment, certainly every medical breakthrough of the last century has involved research with animals. Without animal research, all of the medical advances of the last century might never have occurred". Such statements are an amalgam of opinion, fallacy and implied necessity, and, as we shall see are repudiated by medical history and common sense.

It was through the use of voluntary human subjects, some of whom paid with their lives, and not animals that we learned to cope with:

> Yellow fever
> Malaria
> Dengue fever
> Round worm
> Tapeworm
> Typhus fever
> Infectious hepatitis
> Small pox

A "Partial listing of Advances Made Without Animals," compiled by the Physicians Committee for Responsible Medicine, also serves to disprove the testimony of The Foundation for Biomedical Research:

• "Discovery of the relationship between cholesterol and heart disease, the number one cause of death for Americans.

• Discovery of the relationship between smoking and cancer, the number two cause of death for Americans.

• Discovery of the relationship between hypertension and stroke, the number three cause of death for Americans.

• Discovery of the causes of trauma, the number four cause of death in the United States, and the measures to prevent

it.
- Elucidation of the causes of many forms of respiratory disease, Americans' number five cause of death.
- Isolation of the AIDS virus.
- Discovery of the mechanism of AIDS transmission.
- Discovery of penicillin and its curative effect on various diseases.
- Development of x-rays."
- "Discovery of the relationship between chemical exposure and birth defects.
- Development of hormonal treatment for cancer of the prostate and breast.
- Interpretation of the genetic code and its function in protein synthesis.
- Production of Humulin, a synthetic copy of human Insulin, which causes few allergic reactions. Humulin is widely available and the product of choice for insulin-dependent diabetics".

These relevant facts contradict the claim made above by the Foundation for Biomedical Research. It could be argued that we can't extrapolate from a few human volunteer examples to the many different and often traumatic research protocols; that volunteers for such procedures would not be available. I would agree that rational volunteers for painful, and protracted procedures would not be plentiful nor would there be many volunteer animals if they had a choice. But the persuasive claim of necessity intercepts such perception. A symbol with such telling influence upon rational people, must itself be dissected.

Given the validity of the physical laws of motion, the orbits of the planets are elliptical, as a matter of physical necessity. If Socrates is a man, and all men are mortal, it follows with logical necessity that Socrates is mortal. Two

Necessity

plus two times six equals twenty four, by mathematical necessity. Philosophers also speak of moral necessity relative perhaps to individual and cultural differences. Life, human or animal, is a necessary condition of everything else. A situation is necessary if it cannot be other than it is. It is necessary that we have food and liquid if we are to live. It is necessary that the sun continues to exist if we are to survive.

As noted above, the FDA said that research on laboratory animals will continue to be necessary in the foreseeable future. The Foundation for Biomedical Research did not use the word necessary, but unequivocally implied that vivisection was necessary by the clause, "...we have no other choice." The data on pages 20-21 indicates clearly enough, that there are alternative, and productive methods in the quest for biomedical knowledge. To claim we... "have no other choice" is deceptive misleading rhetoric. And such misrepresentation is but the beginning, and not the whole of wrongdoing.

The quest for biomedical knowledge through vivisection, occurs in the realm of contingent events, in which nothing happens of necessity. Competitive events such as baseball football, or a journey to another country, or to the moon, or to town for groceries all take place in the realm of contingent events where nothing happens of necessity.

We are vaguely aware of that realm. But unlike the realm of physical, logical, and mathematical necessity, it is the world of ever present uncertainty: a world in which the unexpected, and often unpredictable is the norm, in which "best laid plans" go wrong, in which love turns to hate, and friends to enemies. It is in this context of contingent events that-a game of chance-research roulette, is played with the bones, guts, skin, organs, blood, and lives of animals, with and without anesthesia. It is a game of chance in which the chips are,(and this is a non exhaustive account) dogs, rats, mice, gerbils, cats, cows, birds, horses, primates, sheep, and pigs. It's a game played every day with no end in sight. It's not only the majority of people that are misled by the vivisector's cry of necessity, that claim also tends to mislead the claimant. As purported in 1993 in "Bioscience," animal tests for toxicity were claimed to be a necessary condition for public safety. That allegation was affirmed by testimony from Paul Silber, who claimed that this century would not produce a satisfactory model on which to perform the LD 50 toxicity test to replace a whole living animal.

It was in the spring of 1997 (this century) that the Physicians Committee for Responsible Medicine announced that,"new cell tests beat animal tests."

Late 1996 brought two long awaited breakthroughs. First, a new study shows that new safety tests using human cells are more accurate than animal tests. Second, a new company offers methods for developing new drugs that use no animals at all.

Researchers from the U.S., Europe, Japan, and other countries tried 68 different test tube- methods to predict the toxicity of 50 different chemicals.... The results were presented at the conference of the Scandinavian Society for Cell Toxicology, in September, 1966. The human cell tests were clearly superior to the mouse and rat tests.

Most ill informed mortals believe that the control of poliomyelitis was the irreplaceable function of animal research. As we shall see, a "Background Paper" published by the Physicians Committee for Responsible Medicine tends to destroy that myth.

THE CONTROL OF POLIO provides an excellent example of the value of careful human clinical investigation. Unfortunately,

Necessity

animal experiments led to number of false conclusions causing the loss of many years' time in the struggle to control the disease. In 1908, Viennese immunologist Karl Landsteiner and his associate Ervin Popper noted that bacteria could not be found in infected human spinal cord tissue, correctly indicating that the cause was a virus. Later Lansteiner turned to animal experimentation, studying the effects of the polio virus on various non-human species who were given the disease artificially.

Unfortunately, these animal experiments directed attention away from the study of the human disease, and wasted researchers time. John R. Paul, historian and scientist at Yale's Poliomyelitis Unit, wrote: Many who followed him became so entangled in the intricacies of research on the experimental infection that they were never able to shake themselves sufficiently loose to explore the human disease.... It was as if some of the main investigators, particularly in the United States, had become so transfixed with the importance of laboratory work on experimental poliomyelitis that they had, for the time being, arrived at the assumption that it was the only type of poliomyelitis research worth doing. The first clues to the means of immunizing against polio came from studies of the natural immunity that occurs in patients recovering from mild polio virus infection. In 1910, researchers at the public health service discovered antibodies to the polio virus in humans who had recovered from the systemic(non-neurologic) illness. In 1912, a team of clinical investigators at the Rockefeller institute found antibodies in healthy people in amounts similar to that in people convalescing from polio. That same year Swedish researcher W. Wernstedt developed the theory of naturally acquired immunity caused by mild, inapparent infection. This meant that exposure to the virus early in life could prevent disease later. His source of information was human epidemiological data.

Although these human studies paved the way for methods to prevent infection, animal experiments continued to misdirect research efforts, and it was to be another 25 years before investigators finally picked up the trail left by clinical researchers. (25 years!)

It was Albert Sabin M.D., who observed during a 1984 House Subcommittee meeting: Work on prevention (of polio) was long delayed by an erroneous conception of the nature of the human disease, based on misleading experimental models of the disease in monkeys. Researchers now recommend cultivating the virus for Salk vaccine production in human connective tissue cells instead of monkey kidney cell preparations. Human cell derived vaccines are just as effective, less expensive, and eliminate the serious danger of animal virus contamination.

W. Hennessen, a professor at the Bureau of Applied Immunology in Bern, Switzerland, notes: It is common knowledge now that test systems became infinitely more sensitive when the animals used were replaced by other methods.

The history of research on polio shows the value of human clinical research and human cell culture techniques. To the extent that animal experiments have been replaced by such methods, the research endeavor has been improved and accelerated.

Sabin vaccine manufacturers still test the vaccine by injecting it into the spinal cords of live monkeys. They use this test to check whether the live vaccine will cause polio, even though this test is time consuming and expensive, and difficult to correlate with effects in humans. The results vary excessively, according to the World Health Organization. Researchers at the National Institute for Biological Standards and Control in London write: The degree of correlation between the neuro-virulence of a poliovirus when inoculated into the central nervous system of a monkey and its safety in man is not known at the present time. Between 1973 and 1984, the Sabin vaccine caused 101 out of 138 cases of paralytic poliomyelitis in the U.S. Reachers have developed a laboratory method of determining neuro-virulence, which may provide a replacement for the monkey test. It is based on the detection of virus mutations commonly associated with increased neuro-virulence.

The history of research on polio shows the value of human clinical research, studies of human tissues, and human cell culture techniques. To the extent that animal experiments have been replaced by such methods, the research endeavor has been improved and accelerated.

The facts as described above pertain to one aspect of a controversial, multifaceted practice made saleable by the expectation of benefits and by the specious cry of necessity. But it must be repeated: The practice of vivisection cannot be classified as either a matter of physical, mathematical or logical necessity. And as we have seen, it cannot be validly described as a necessary condition of discovery. Helpless animals unable to defend themselves became victimized because they were considered to be expendable, and the expendable, available, and instrumental became conveniently defined as the necessary.

We need not and can not expose every link in the causal chain that is responsible for this methodical and vicious practice of human tyranny. Obvious links would include well publicized results in which animals were instrumental, monetary gain by avaricious individuals, academic ambitions, public apathy born of ignorance of the horrible facts, the expectation of benefits by a hopeful public and the cry of necessity. All of these factors served to sustain the acceptance of vivisection and perhaps repressed to a marked degree, incentive for the creation of nonviolent acceptable methods. Overlooked, or unknown, were other very relevant facts. Neither gruesome procedures, nor numerous failures, made headlines--nor the expenditure of vast sums of money- and most importantly the extent of suffering and death forced on the animal kingdom. Thus our collective practical judgement was formed by slivers of the truth and not the whole unspeakable truth.

What a spokesperson for the vivisection enterprise would reply to the above is not known, but we can speculate: "The world will not come to an end if vivisection is abolished, but prospects for advances in medicine will diminish in that event." That prophesy would beg the question, while implying necessity.

In the words of the Swiss historian Jacob Burkhardt: "A future known in advance is an absurdity." Our question-begging spokesperson might also argue that "the vivisector knows that his research is a practice where nothing happens of necessity, and that he may or may not find what he is looking for in the entrails of animals."

We are here in the presence of a hypothetical attempt to vindicate an alleged "necessary" but immoral game of research roulette in which live animals are the chips: and the player is very much aware that what he seeks may or may not be found.

The allegation of necessity then, *that can not be proven by empirical evidence* became the master, and billions of helpless animals the sacrificial "models," truth, compassion, and morality be damned! All of which can not happen in an isolated social vacuum. Based on what seems to be a valid correlation between cruelty to animals and people, it could well be that the abolition of the most long lived methodical cruelty as now practiced, would eventually lead to a less violent and crime plagued world via a means end continuum.

The transition would spell the end of wholesale brutality, and free massive amounts of money, which if prudently used, would benefit mankind infinitely more than the barbarism displaced. Thus hideous merciless procedures, from Galen's dissection of nonhuman primates without anesthesia, to the burn experiments of the Pentagon, would be relegated to the history of medical abominations.

5
Partisan Versus Partisan
Part One

One man's word is no word: We shall quietly hear both sides.
                                                        Goethe

Had the poet foreseen the unending confrontation between Partisans, and partisans, he may have said: "Be aware when you speak on behalf of animals, that from no point in time can the unknown horrors that they suffered be made known, because the invisible cannot be made visible." That insight would bespeak a continuum from prehistoric times to the ubiquitous tyrannizing of animals in the last year of the twentieth century.

Thus any brief for animals must be a severely truncated account of realities and there can be no Nuremberg day of reckoning. "Probability," as noted by Bertrand Russell, "is always relative to relevant data." The data with which we are here concerned is the human abuse and killing of billions upon billions of animals, which will probably continue unabated sans rational humane intervention. As noted above, there can be no tribunal for animals, but that doesn't preclude the dissemination of truth, and responsible opinion based on the quest for justice, to counter fallacy, and irresponsible opinion.

We shall, in the following pages, "quietly hear both sides" in a manner calculated to accurately reflect the thoughts of partisans, whose identities (with some exceptions) **will not be made public.**

Partisan Versus Partisan *Part One*

Unfortunately, truth is not always a corollary of sincerity, a disparity exemplified by Mr. Journalist's frequent defense of vivisection.

His use of the testimony of the famous and knowledgeable Dr.partisan is impressive, but such evidence is not always irrefutable. Dr.partisan dogmatically claimed that there is no substitute for the use of animals in medical research. His claim is not a value judgement, but a judgement about a matter of fact that is either true or false. It is not only false, but reveals an unscientific attitude because it begs the question, and speaks with certainty, which is contrary to the scientific spirit. That spirit eschews certainty in favor of probability in view of known facts.

My concern about the biomedical research that preceded successful coronary bypass graft surgery prompted me to contact former vivisector John McArdle Ph.D., member of the advisory panel to the Congress of the United States Office of Technology Assessment. In his response June 26,1987 he wrote:

All of the others did use animals, but that was a reflection of how primitive biomedical research was at the time, and does not prove that animals are needed to answer biomedical questions today. The real alternatives for such work today are clinical studies on sick animals and humans, and the use of clinically brain-dead human cadavers, which are available and are being used at some university hospitals.

"I am troubled," wrote Irwin D. Bros Ph.D., by a paradox in cancer research today. On one hand, we have sophisticated scientific instruments, computers, and the elegant language of modern mathematics available for medical research. On the other hand, the ritual slaughter of animals continues to be practiced. This ritual slaughter can serve little or no scientific purpose for mutagenic diseases such as cancer." "We are," claimed The New England Journal of Medicine, "losing the war against cancer."

The foregoing testimony by Dr. McArdle and Dr. Bross, as well as that of the New England Journal of Medicine, does not prove Dr. partisan's contention to be erroneous. But such evidence does serve to underscore the lack of complete accord by respected authorities on a question of vital importance. The criterion for determining the validity of Dr. partisan testimony lies in the investigation of its literal truth. One counter instance proves it to be false. Pages 20 and 21 above of section 4 provide considerably more than one counter instance, and makes it clear that partisan testimony is not valid. We can best understand the graveness of such error, in terms of the horror rituals that endorsement implies.

These rituals are more than an important controversial issue. They are the source of mutilation, suffering, and killing of animals on the one hand and the constant anguish of grief inflicted on concerned people on the other hand. The latter anguish, which is of secondary importance, will terminate only when the former ritual of horror is no longer tolerated: Abolished.

Partisan Versus Partisan *Part One*

How can a sane person object to and wish to do away with medical testing that is in the interest of people? Thus agonized Mr. partisan. His attempt to characterize a humane and moral outlook as something irrational is a paradigm of self- deceptive obtuseness. He is certain of the rightness of his beliefs, and implies that Partisans have no moral right to speak or act as they do on behalf of animals, and that there is one, and only one method of medical testing in the interest of people. We don't have a moral right to be crusaders for what we believe to be the true and the good? Paul of Tarsus wouldn't agree with Mr. partisan; neither would Moses, Martin Luther, or the late Martin Luther King Jr.

"Like man," wrote partisan "animals are unique, but does that logically lead to the conclusion that they are sacrosanct, that they must be totally protected from man?"

The *logical* conclusion that animals (or man) are sacrosanct, cannot be derived from facts apparent or real, because of the unbridgeable *logical* gulf between empirical facts and moral judgements. And-contrary to what is dogmatically claimed-we can't *logically* conclude that animals do or do not have soul.

To cite the obvious, animals must be protected from man, by man, for the same reason that the environment must be his constant concern: because there is no alternative other than the agents responsible for the wrongdoing. That the obvious must be cited, is another of the dismal facts of life.

Partisan Versus Partisan *Part One*

The argument for vivisection as presented by Alfred partisan and other advocates of vivisection is based upon the generalization that the practice is an unmitigated blessing. Such arguments seek what in the very nature of the case cannot be obtained: unqualified scientific affirmation and moral sanction.

According to partisan, animal research is by and large a humane practice in which animals are treated well. The perusal of relevant literature will convince one with an open mind that this partisan's testimony is outrageously misleading.

Anesthesia is incompatible with many post-operative observations:

With experiments on the nervous system.
Or pain or behavior or stress.
Or all experiments of long duration.
Or all those that induce any disease,
for the purpose of studying it.
Or with the preventive efficacy, and
toxicity of all new drugs.

Anesthesia is usually administered to animals prior to a serious surgical procedure and mainly to keep them still. But since the animal is totally immobilized by a restraining device, and solidly muzzled, or surgically devocalized, there is no way to show any discomfort or severe pain. And nobody knows how effectively, and for how long the animal is unconscious.

Arguments to defend such barbarism are calculated to ensure acceptance and avoid censure. Thus we are told that nearly all discovery in human and animal health care, can be attributed to a great degree on animal research. Such words can mean anything proclivity wishes them to mean. My reading of medical history is less ambiguous. It is there that we learn that clinical observation and epidemiological studies account for most of what we know to sustain human health and prolong life.

The unspeakable things we have done to billions of animals as if they were unfeeling stones did elicit some knowledge, which is not to say *there was no other way.* But another way was not an attractive option in a world with no shortage of helpless animals and people who could benefit academically and economically from their vile exploitation, as uninformed publics silently consented to what they could not, and would not bear to witness.

Partisan Versus Partisan *Part One*

Professor Edward Zorn's article "Animal Lovers and Misanthropes" is in the main at odds with the facts, but the facts exist regardless of what anyone thinks of them. "It is a commonplace of biological research," the Report of the British Pharmaceutical Industry's expert committee on drug toxicity has admitted, "that information from one animal species cannot be taken as valid for any other."

Zorn has characterized Partisans ("animal advocates") as "man haters," which is an *ad hominem* (name calling) attack. The animal rights movement is based on the premise, claims Zorn, that animals must be protected even if it means that people must suffer and die. Can we believe that several hundred thousand Partisans and Albert Schweitzer, who admonished the world to not impose suffering on animals, can be credibly classified as misanthropes? Myth refuses to be eluded; here we find it in a professor's irresponsible words. Zorn the professor is also a prophet. He predicts that many human beings will perish if vivisection is terminated. The prediction is not in the form of a well qualified opinion but of irrefutable dogma. He can not *know* that many people will perish because of the termination of vivisection because that knowledge is not *logically* derivable from any combination of facts.

Animals are crying and screaming all over the world because of such speculation and the inertia of a world that perceives it as unquestionable truth.

Partisan Versus Partisan *Part One*

Ms. Journalist is allegedly an animal lover, and her latest rhetoric makes one question the validity of that claim. People, she says, don't like to torture animals this way. What way, did a paragraph get lost?

By "this way," the lady means: Take a few albino rabbits, confine them to restraining hutches with only their heads showing, and pull the lower lid away from the eyeball of each rabbit to form a cup. Into this cup drop a few milligrams of whatever it is to be tested for toxicity, hold the rabbit's eye closed for one second and then let it go. A day later come back to see if the lids are swollen, the iris inflamed, the cornea ulcerated, or the rabbit blinded in that eye.

Alternatively, their eyes may be permanently held open by the use of metal clips,which keep the eyelids apart,in which case the rabbits can obtain no relief at all from the burning irritation of the substance placed in their eyes. As Ms. Journalist explained, people don't like to torture animals in this way. And I must ask, why do they? One must have reasons to not condemn, but defend such procedures, and Ms. Journalist did have two reasons.

1)   She believes that in the foreseeable future there will probably be improvements in various cosmetics and household products. 2)Kids tend to eat cosmetics and even drink shampoo or cologne.

We can be sure that unrelenting competition will foster improvements, but how that can justify what they do to animals is perhaps clear to Ms. Journalist, but not to this Partisan. It is quite clear however that giant corporations would not spend huge sums of their precious money to torture animals, if they did not deem it to be in their interest to do so, i.e., interest defined as necessity in a litigious world. The animals can only scream, and struggle, but a scream that is not heard can't awaken a somnolent world.

Partisan Versus Partisan *Part One*

Concerned Partisans however, could be heard and seen when they demonstrated, as reported in Peter Singer's "Animal Liberation," second edition.

And, it is very clear, Ms. Journalist, that what was once a routine ritual of torture by Mary Kay, Avon, Amway, Revlon, Faberge, is apparently no longer deemed necessary, from which it follows that our mercenary, vain, caustic, toxic one-way trip through hell for animals exemplified the power of the untrue plea of necessity.

Partisan Versus Partisan *Part One*

One of our persistent beliefs is that we humans are morally superior to all other forms of sentient life that, in self contradiction, we routinely brutalize. Thus proponents of vivisection often have their day in the mass media, which cannot be said for their frustrated opposition.

"I'm a lover of dogs," says Detective Jones, "but not an antivivisectionist. I think experiments on animals is a necessary evil." "Perhaps," replies Officer Plennik, "but not on my poodle."

Is vivisection "evil," and "necessary" as Jones claims? The cop is not entirely wrong. If it's "evil" to sometimes burn, cut, crush, poison and microwave live animals, with and without anesthesia, then vivisection is "evil." But the relevant contrary evidence tends to refute the claim of "necessary" as a condition of medical discovery and knowledge.

Jones is a good cop, but betrays his ignorance of the contradiction entailed in his declaration of love for dogs, and sanction of vivisection as a "necessary evil." From the time of the tyrants of Rome until the tyrants of our not so brave new world, necessity has been an instrument of persuasion and influence, and the concept still works. Officer Plennik's emotional display of selective concern for his poodle is a paradigm of stunted and seemingly moral concern.

A stray dog, or cat, or unloved pig trapped in a laboratory cage, can be subjected to as much agony as a beloved poodle. However, to perceive an animal to which we have a strong emotional attachment as something special, not to be one of millions of animals condemned to the research mill is a common, if not the predominant attitude.

But, why should another animal that we have never seen, whose cries we can't hear, not also warrant our concern and compassion? Is that which we don't experience but are vaguely of, nonexistent and not worthy of our concern and compassion?

Partisan Versus Partisan *Part One*

Dr. partisans' article maintains that the anti-vivisectionist position is erroneous because it is sullied by emotion. He insisted moreover, that the vivisection issue does not entail the rights of animals, or the take-home pay of scientists, but is simply an issue of human health and well-being. Can we indiscriminately equate emotionalism with error? Can we reduce the controversial subject of vivisection solely to the issue of human health and well-being? A mothers love for a child, a child's love for a parent, the feeling of elation imparted by beauty in its myriad forms -all are examples of positive emotions that can not be classified as error. And not all negative emotions such as hate, fear, outrage, and rage can be called error because of the possibility of justification of such gut reactions.

Emotionalism can lead one astray, but it can also intensify understanding. A measure of emotion apropos of the evils of vivisection is a prerequisite, if language is to reflect to more than a degree the reality of such horrors. To label burning, blinding, gassing, poisoning, fracturing, cutting, drowning, crushing, and the whole hideous inventory of cruelties that constitute vivisection as merely an issue of human health, and well being, is crude anthropocentric fiction. I have an interest in health and well-being and I love life. But I would not defile myself by advocating the vivisectors' hell for reasons of health, well being and long life, not even with a guarantee from the vivisection enterprise.

Dr. partisan's negative allusion to the take-home pay of scientists is not a self evident truth the human pursuit of interest has prevailed, and will continue to do so ad infinitum. And that pursuit is a causal factor, that contributes to a significant degree to the vivisection enterprise. In the words of George Washington,

..Few men are capable of making continual sacrifice of all views of interest or

Partisan Versus Partisan *Part One*

advantage to the common good. It is vain to exclaim against the depravity of human nature on this account; the fact is so, as the experience of every age and nation has proved it and we must in a great measure change the constitution of man before we can make it otherwise.

Such words bring to mind what we know, but tend to forget, and are applicable to both saints, and sinners of medicine and science.

There can be no denying that people often exhibit emotion when discussing vivisection. And there can be no denying that there are vivisectors working for what they believe to be in the interest of the race, in a manner not perceived as evil. And there can be no denying, that there are vivisectors who have left the laboratory to crusade against it, because they believe it to be an immoral abomination. Because animals, as well as humans, have a property in themselves there can be no shirking the conclusion, that animals have a moral right to not be the property of, or relentlessly tyrannized by humans, from which it follows that they should have a statutory right unambiguously reflecting that fact.

Partisan Versus Partisan *Part One*

Is it unethical or immoral to call attention to the horrors of vivisection in the research laboratory? Mr. partisan thinks so, because doing so has contributed to the cost of doing business for those involved in research, resulting in less productivity. Therefore, we are instructed to say to someone who has lost a loved one to disease: Better him or her than some rodent. And if you should encounter a child incapacitated by some debilitative disease, hold his gaze while telling him: "Let us not hurt and kill animals so that you can be healthy!" Such advice is partisan's derisive way of making a point, namely, that Partisans are utterly wrongheaded.

"And let us not forget" says Mr. partisan "all life is precious, but human life is by far the most precious, because a human life has more intrinsic value than a monkey's life."

I would agree that I am a more precious organism than a monkey, but I am not at all sure a monkey would concur. But I am sure that an articulate man-eating tiger would take issue with partisan's thesis. Ergo, I am not sure that the concept of value is absolute, and not relative to the judgement of the deciding being.

From the vantage point of many, if not most, people, they and their kind are of most value, and valued the most. Animals are not capable of ethnocentrism, anthropocentrism, or nationalism, but do exhibit an affinity for their own kind. And, I believe that we can infer from the principle of self love as a helpful instrument of self preservation, that we humans don't hold a monopoly of egoism. When we assert that a human being has greater intrinsic value than an animal, we are giving expression to our own emotions, not to a self evident truth. As Bertrand Russell observed, "questions as to values lie wholly outside the domain of knowledge." If one's value (preciousness) is not an absolute, but relative to

Partisan Versus Partisan *Part One*

the judgement of the decision maker, we need an objective criterion if we wish to accurately determine whom to banish to protracted misery and pain in the research lab. The avoidance of subjectivity lies in the creation of a preciousness gauge! If a senile grandmother shows up a few grams short of the right stuff, off she goes. Will they accept an ex-president? Or idiotic adults or children? Or pathological pedophiles? Or serial killers?

There are certainly enough unfortunate beings around to provide all sorts of transplant spare parts, and those who fail to pass muster needn't despair, Mr. partisan. Perhaps souls,(not flesh and bone,) are impervious to scalpels, saws, drills, caustic chemicals etc., and will confound the vivisectors invasive investigation and find peace in another world.

Partisan Versus Partisan *Part One*

"Animal research done with compassion and kindness," wrote Dr. J.E. partisan, "has saved the lives of millions of animals, and people."

An environment of caged animals, with its irrefutable evidence of trauma, fear, stress, and suffering is not an aggregate of compassion, and kindness, but of insensitive human callousness. To characterize the research ritual and slaughter as compassionate and kind is misleadingly fallacious. The "millions of animals and people" claim, is a club that can dash reason asunder, and ipso facto the abominable becomes humane and good and must be sustained at any cost. But to conclude that the abominable, attractively described is to be sanctioned, does not follow with **logical necessity** from the alleged facts. In the words of Professor Stuart Hampshire who taught at Oxford University, "Certainly no practical judgement is **logically** deducible from any set of statements of facts...." The vivisection enterprise, in other words, is not predicated on a foundation of logical reasoning, but on a biological science version of medieval torture to extract information and is misleadingly characterized as entailing compassion and kindness.

Partisan Versus Partisan *Part One*

Mr. Journalist believes that vivisectors must have the right to use stray animals, not pets, to find cures for diseases, and to develop better surgical skills. This gent callously suggests at the outset that we have a moral, as well as legal, right to banish animals to the vivisection lab. If Mr. Journalist were to suggest the use of idiotic, deformed, and indigent people in medical research, who can experience pain and suffer, we would correctly label him as a media lunatic.

Is a stray animal born without a central nervous system enabling the animal to *not* experience pain and suffer, or endowed in that manner by strayness? Upon the answer to that question we find one of the various reasons to reject Mr. Journalist's suggestion.

Another of the various tragic ramifications of the vivisection business is the theft of thousands of "pets," labeled as strays, which for a price become models on the researcher's stainless table. And we will never know how many beloved companion animals or abandoned strays suffered and died on that bloodied table.

Partisan Versus Partisan *Part One*

Mr. partisan questions the earnestness of Partisans who criticize the vivisection enterprise. His acid test would be their behavior when in need of medical or surgical treatment developed through the use of animals. Refusal, he believes, would confirm their sincerity, and acceptance their hypocrisy. He also argues that the fate of everyone would be in grave peril if vivisection were abolished. Mr. partisan's proposal of trial by behavior is a variation of two stale queries conceived by present-day inquisitors apparently opposed to, and annoyed by Partisan ideology. A)Are your shoes made of leather? B) Are you a vegetarian?

This vegetarian still wears leather shoes because he could not find (and the search will continue) satisfactory plastic substitutes. Speaking only for myself: Acceptance of medical treatment (with the exception of xenotransplantation which I could not submit to) could not extinguish the injustice suffered by animals in the past. But refusal urged by principle, might jeopardize my ability to contribute to the creation of a new standard of justice for animals.

To predict that we would be collectively endangered by the abolition of vivisection is to indirectly sanction its continuation by virtue of necessity: The tyrant's plea! That strategy is not justified, and can't be logically derived from any combination of facts. This partisan's prediction, based perhaps on relevant knowledge, is speculative, and a non sequitur. One can speculate but no one can divine the consequences of the abolition of unceasing tyranny in the name of justice.

It would be rash to predict that a world that had divorced itself from the second oldest profession, the brutal exploitation of animals, might become the best of all possible worlds for all sentient life. But that possibility, I believe, warrants serious deliberation.

6

Partisan Versus Partisan

Part Two

Goethe's dictum will be observed within practical limitations by the following testimony from both sides of the dispute. The partisan comments will be followed by a critical concluding Partisan response to each partisan segment, with the exception of partisan segment's number one and two, which will elicit but one response.

Partisan Versus Partisan *Part Two*

(1)   The mouse model created at Northwestern University In Chicago, for use in research on amyotrophic lateral sclerosis Lew Gehrig's disease, was the source of Dr. Mark E. Gurney's optimistic pro vivisection comments.

(2)   Dr. H. Cohen of Northwestern University, author of "Necessary Science" publicly observed that many major research universities had become the target of Partisan's, intent on putting an end to the machinations in the animal research lab. His defense of five Northwestern scientists included the following descriptions of the ends sought:
A)Early diagnosis of diseases,   such as glaucoma) Information relevant to diseases such as muscular degeneration, a blinding disease.) The search for knowledge of abnormal brain circuits underlying epileptic seizures. D)Studies to determine the relation of brain to speech disorders. He also provided a micro medical history of the accomplishments of vivisection and indicated that there is often no alternative to animal models to achieve victory over disease. The sole purpose of biological research was claimed to be the acquisition of knowledge to facilitate diagnosis and treatment prevent disease, relieve suffering, and   save and extend life.

Response
(1) (2) There are only a few pro vivisection, apologies as exemplified above by Dr.Gurney and Dr. Cohen, variations of which have been told over and over again. The above incomplete examples by medical doctors display different approaches to achieve the same result: the perpetuation of vivisection. An *informative* brief for vivisection would cite not only achievements and objectives, but also the procedures to be used, lucidly described in laity terms. An **uninformative** brief for vivisection   would cite achievements or objectives, but

not a gruesome word about procedures: Why? because there can be no credible defense for a human-imposed routine torture and death of countless animals in any context.

(3)"Why Animal Experimentation Should Continue" is the title of an essay written by sophomore Karl Bierm. His opinions include the necessity in the foreseeable future of animals in experimental research to discover cures for AIDS and cystic fibrosis. It should continue because it has been the means through which all modern vaccinations have been developed, from which animals have also benefited. It should continue for people who suffer incurable diseases or disabilities, who hope for a cure through research that requires the use of animals. Finally, he suggests that people should consider the question of whether the welfare of laboratory animals is more important than the combined members of humanity and the rest of the animal kingdom.

Response
(3)   A proposition is either true or false. If it is true that President Lincoln was assassinated in a theatre, it was true yesterday, as it is true today, and will be true tomorrow. It is true that some people suffer from incurable afflictions as alleged by Biern, and if incurable literally means not curable, their afflictions will be not be curable for the rest of their lives. I sympathize with such people, which is not to say as Biern implies, that hope and despair justifies the atrocities of vivisection. Hope and despair don't justify the mutilation and death of animals for the same reason that they don't justify the mutilation, and death of millions of people.   If, telling evidence to the contrary, vaccines were proven to be an unmitigated blessing, it would not follow with logical necessity that only through vivisection could vaccines be developed.

Partisan Versus Partisan *Part Two*

Biern's leading question implies that the welfare of humanity and the animal kingdom is contingent upon vivisection, for which there is no evidence. Contrary to what Biern would have us believe the welfare of humanity could be better served by diverting the billions spent on vivisection to the needs of the sick and hungry people of the world, concomitant with an ongoing educational program delineating the requirements of a healthy and relatively disease-free life style.

(4)   The pages of the **Readers Digest** extolled the virtues of vivisection and attempted to depreciate the humane position of its Partisan opposition. Thus the critique was accentuated apropos of purpose. Enemies such as diabetes, smallpox, diphtheria, measles, whooping cough, polio, and rubella allegedly capitulated to the assault of the vivisectors. Also cited was control of infection by antibiotics achieved by the same assault.

Benefits to animals allegedly included: open heart surgery, cataract surgery, cardiac pace makers, and immunization against rabies, distemper, feline leukemia, tetanus, and anthrax.

Dr. Lewis Thompson maintained, in effect, that animal research was a necessary condition of progress in medical science. How will people react, queried Dr. Michael E. De Bakey, to the statutory rights of animals above those of humans? And Dr. Louis W. Sullivan, Secretary of the Department of Health and Human Services, also provided testimony for the seven pages of "The Animal Rights War on Medicine" in **The Readers Digest.**

Response

(4) To define animal rights as a "War on Medicine" as the **Readers Digest** article did, is deceptively misleading. The

animal rights movement is, as I understand it, a war on the human tyranny of animals in any context; not a war on medicine. Dr. De Bakey wanted to know how people will react to the statutory rights of animals above that of humans. This is a loaded question indicating the intention and the attitude of the questioner. The most intelligent animal can never have the rights enjoyed by humans, with but two exceptions, i.e., the right to not be the property of humans; the right to not be tyrannized by humans. These are not rights above that of humans, but are rights equivalent to that of humans to not be owned, bought, sold, or tyrannized by humans. I am acquainted with only a fraction of the thousands of "animal people," but have learned in approximately twenty years that they are not anti-medicine ideologues. I would characterize them as people vehemently opposed to the tyrannization of animals, for any reason.

Here again we find the uninformative defense of vivisection citing achievement only, but not a giving a lucid word about procedures. How many and what kind of animals were used? How many lived and how many died? Prudent evaluation without such relevant information is impossible. To know of one's accomplishments is not always a criterion for evaluation. If a person becomes very wealthy through robbery, torture, and murder, does his or her vast wealth justify the means in a society governed by the rule of law? Means and ends, as Aristotle believed, consist of one indivisible whole.

Yes, knowledge has been gleaned from vivisection, a fact from which we can't logically deduce the necessity of vivisection, now or in the past. But we can logically deduce that animals used as human analogs were enough like their tormentors, as evidenced by their use, to have an inviolable property in themselves, which we have persisted, and do persist in violating.

As with any ethical concept, common sense can't be overruled. To dispatch a raging or rabid animal to avert human or non human disaster should not be prohibited. But to tyrannize or kill an animal in the name of recreation or science, or to consume an animal's flesh, excluding subsistence food, should be, I believe, unlawful. An ethical code needed for a much less ferocious world would embody these precepts, and would be in the long term, in the best interests of both humans and animals.

(5)   Those who read **Glamour's** January, 1990 issue may remember that Jerod M. Loeb Ph.D., director of the division of biomedical science for the A.M.A., would be shocked if vivisection was not responsible for some progress in AIDS research, in which chimps were used as models.

He also seemed to be certain that the reduction of heart disease and childhood leukemia couldn't have happened without the use of animals. As of this moment, he noted, vivisection is providing valuable data about pancreatic transplants and a vaccine for chicken pox. The testimony of Steve Carrol, a member of a group called Incurably Ill for Animal Research, revealed his opinion based on personal experience. Having been severely burned in an accident, he doesn't think he would be alive had there not existed various techniques developed through vivisection. The questions in the article that must be here included were: Faced with the choice of saving human, or animal lives, how do we choose? And, is an animals life of greater importance than the life of your child?

Response
(5)   The "Incurably Ill for Animal Research" includes Steve Carrol. Steve was severely burned in an accident, and doesn't

Partisan Versus Partisan *Part Two*

think he would be alive, had there not existed various techniques available due to vivisection. Thus belief sired desire for the perpetuation of vivisection. Carrol's support of vivisection is an example of the tendency to interpret justice in terms of self interest on the one hand, and the immoral practice of bifurcating means and ends on the other hand (which Aristotle would not have sanctioned). This Partisan perceives the objective and the means employed --vivisection-- as an inseparable unacceptable whole made immoral by the means. This is not to imply that the goal of health and well-being should be relegated to the realm of the unattainable. You forget, says necessity with a smirk, I am not only the tyrants plea: I am also the parent of invention.

It won't do to dodge the closing hackneyed questions, which are: A) Faced with the choice of saving human or animal lives, how do we choose? B) Is an animals life of greater importance than the life of your child? Reversing the order of the above: B) Let me not be told that the life of any child, or animal is more important to me than my child. And A) let us not be intimidated by false dilemmas, as posed by the first question. Thousands, perhaps tens of thousands of third world children die each week from various afflictions; thousands of children in India go blind each year due to insufficient protein.

Many men, women, and children on planet earth (which includes America) perish every year because of preventable diseases and malnutrition. A few dimes per day will feed a very hungry child in the third world, of which there are millions. The speculative predictions of the provivisection people entailing the brutal equivalent of the rack, thumb screws, the iron maiden, flaying, and burning may or may not prove to be valid. But if preventing suffering and saving lives is the goal in this myopic world we can divert the huge sums of money that vivisection consumes in the process of brutalizing and destroying animals, to the humane business of saving millions of people from suffering, blindness, and death, and millions, if not billions, of animals from tyranny and death.

(6)   He is an animal rights activist, has argued against cruel research procedures on animals, has a secondhand human heart, which he believes was made possible by research on animals. He also believes that animal organs may, in the future, also replace hearts, livers, maybe lungs and he has a question: If a Partisan needed a transplant, would he or she refuse the organ of an animal if nothing else were available?

Response
(6) The alleged "animal rights activist" with a transplanted human heart had a good question. If a Partisan needed a transplant, would he or she refuse the organ of an animal if nothing else were available? This Partisan answers with a question: Could I continue to strive for justice for animals from the grave? I could not. But I would not accept the heart of another animal, and I would use whatever time I had left to continue in the quest for a less ferocious world, sans animals or animal parts for sale.

(7)   "In the last analysis," said Dr. Brill,"the public will not be willing to abandon animal research and resign itself to Alzheimers and AIDS. Sure, there is a cost to research, but there is another concern--humans. And we will always value them more than animals."

Response
(7) I agree that we will always value humans more than animals. But we don't know that vivisection is a necessary con-

dition of the cure for AIDS, which is in essence what Brill is saying. And we do know, and it is relevant, that Dr. Sabin testified to a 1984 House Subcommittee that: "Work on prevention of polio was long delayed by an erroneous conception of the nature of the human disease, based on misleading experimental models of the disease on monkeys." And we do know that it is the unprovable cry of necessity that has sustained tyrannous vivisection on helpless animals which, as with involuntary people, we have no moral right to be doing.

(8) The writer's son was born with a bioplastic left heart. Four years of open heart surgery, and all that entails, produced (we hope) a viable human. And he wishes to know: Is there an animal advocate that can equate the life of his son with the lives of a thousand rats?

Response

(8) Is there a Partisan that can equate the life of this mans' son with the lives of a thousand rats? This incomplete question is calculated to confound the Partisan antivivisectionist, whose answer would be construed to indicate ideological error. I must answer with a question. Would the loving parent with the rat question equate the life of his son with the lives of millions of starving, dying, children desperately in need of the food and medical attention that money can buy? Money that keeps the vivisection enterprise in business? Or are such pathetic children as unimportant as the mice, cats, horses, cows, pigs, primates, reptiles, birds, and other beings that can burn in the fires of vivisection, which is the missing part of his question.

(9) Mr. Journalist's comforting assurance tends to assuage the anxiety of people with companion animals, while invoking

an unintended reality. No, he affirms, your pooch won't be sent to the slaughterhouse, but we can't give stray dogs and cats a pass. That would not be in our interest.

Response

(9) This writers insensitive allusion to a slaughterhouse reveals a part of the truth about the vivisection laboratory obscured by language and his callous distinction between stray and companion animals provides a glimpse of his own portrait. The vivisection laboratory is, in effect, with some exceptions, a slaughterhouse entailing preliminary procedures defined as research, which is an inadequate definition. Perhaps the following definition will be considered for an informative word book. Vivisection laboratory: Research facility for the biomedical use of animal models which, like man, exhibit physical, intellectual, and perceptual faculties, emotions such as affection, attachment, fear, joy, and depression, and the capacity to experience pain and suffering.

All of these traits apply to farm animals, abandoned or stolen companion animals, strays, and animals born and raised to be experimental models.

In the envisioned Partisan world of tomorrow, there will not be thousands of sick, starving, stray cats or dogs, no slaughterhouses euphemistically labeled as research labs, and no killing venues labeled slaughterhouses.

(10) If "Half a loaf is better than none," so is the New York attorney's eclectic humane concern manifest in his partisan rhetoric. The abattoir: A barbaric institution. Calves taken from their mothers to become veal: An abomination. The Draize test: vicious. But stop all experiments on animals, heaven forbid! Didn't Surgeon General Enders say that to stop vivisection is to forget about a cure for AIDS?. Animal

advocates (Partisans) must ask themselves: Is the life of an animal worth more than a human's life? If death of a child could be prevented only through the use of an untested procedure, which could also be dangerous, who should be the volunteer, the child or a laboratory animal? And, said the New York attorney, Partisans are making medical decisions that involve everyone. They may save animal lives while destroying human lives, which we must not allow them to do.

Response

(10) The blinding smoke of rhetoric tends to becloud the issue: it is not known that "scientific" tyranny is the necessary and sufficient condition of a cure for AIDS. And, it's not clear how it can be known that "an untested procedure" could save the life of a child. A child cannot be morally accepted as a volunteer for vivisection, and an animal can't volunteer, and should not be an involuntary model with or without anesthesia. But non-exhaustive possibilities could include the brain dead, and well compensated voluntary "death row" inmates.

The attorney's question: Is the life of an animal worth more than a human life is an example of what Mr. Justice Frankfurter called "the great either or." It is an improper question, a tool of the demagogue attempting to make people take sides in black and white terms, as if there was a simple answer to a complex life and death issue. Nonetheless, the question must be answered.

In this Partisan's scale of values, the life of a person is, by and large, of greater value than that of an animal. And if "greater value" were an unqualified criterion, we could condemn any form of life, perceived as inferior to a lab cage. But animals as well as attorneys have, in our human societal structure, an inviolable property in their respective selves, which should prohibit any and all attempts to tyrannize them, which must include their use as involuntary experimental "guinea pigs."

As to the attorneys last accusation: A proposition is either true or false. Where can the evidence be found that Partisans are "making medical decisions that involve everyone." And that "they may save animal lives while destroying human lives?" There are many Partisans that are Medical Doctors that routinely make medical decisions on behalf of their patients, which never "involve everyone." The lay Partisan practice of medicine and "making of medical decisions" does not exist and is legally and morally prohibited.

I agree that probably millions or billions of animal lives will be saved by the abolition of vivisection. But evidence that human lives would be destroyed can't be found because it doesn't exist. It's true that Partisans wish to save animals from the horrors of vivisection, but it's also true that Mr. attorney's inference from that fact--the destruction of human life is a non sequitur and an attempt to sustain a practical judgement, i.e.,the perpetuation of vivisection. But if such judgements were deducible from the relevant facts, they would be redundant and we could confine ourselves to the facts. This attorney's defense of the still legal abomination labeled vivisection is comparable to the Nazi defense of legal but immoral research on "inferior" people and the defense of legal, but immoral slave trade. War intervened, but I don't think legality could have saved such barbarism indefinitely because of the human proclivity to eventually reject what is perceived to be a flagrant violation of justice. And vivisection and its various savage ramifications is a flagrant violation of justice, which the blinding smoke of rhetoric cannot obscure indefinitely.

Partisan Versus Partisan

Concluding Comments

A Bioscience article proclaimed that animal tests for toxicity were a necessary condition of public safety. Paul Silber president of In Vitro Technologies, claimed that we would not have in this century anything to replace a live animal to perform the LD 50 toxicity test, a scientific word group that doesn't transmit the horror of the test, which evolved in the 1920s. This "science" entails feeding the animals inedible material either mixed with their food, or force fed via a tube down their throats to discover the quantity of the substance that will kill 50% of the animals. The ordeal can last from two weeks to six months for the animals that are still alive, and no animal of the estimated several million used each year is humanely euthanized.

While writing the above, I was trying to recall the words of Oliver Cromwell when he addressed the wary clerics, which I will paraphrase. I beseech you, Mr. Silber, in the bowels of Christ, think it possible that you are mistaken. The prestigious publication Good Medicine, Spring 1997, published by Physicians Committee for Responsible Medicine, provided the following enlightening data.
NEW CELL TESTS BEAT ANIMAL TESTS
Animal tests have come under repeated and deserved criticism for failing to predict dangerous
EFFECTS OF DRUGS AND OTHER CHEMICALS. OF 19 CHEMICALS KNOWN TO CAUSE CANCER IN HUMANS, ONLY SEVEN CAUSED CANCER IN STANDARD ANIMAL TESTS.

Partisan Versus Partisan *Concluding Comments*

The cancer causing effect of chemicals vary so dramatically between species that tests on rats yield different answers from tests on mice for one in every three chemicals tested, according to researchers from Carnegie - Mellon University. Using rodent tests to predict effects in humans is risky at best.

Animal tests routinely miss toxic effects of drugs. The U.S. General accounting office reported that, of all new drugs that entered the market between 1976 and 1985, 52% proved to be more dangerous than animal tests and limited human studies had predicted--so much so that they had to be relabeled with warnings or pulled from the market.

Late 1996 brought two long awaited breakthroughs. First, a new study shows that tests using human cells are more accurate than animal tests. Second, a new company offers methods for developing new drugs that use no animals at all. In the Multi-center Evaluation of In Vitro Cytotoxicity tests (MEIC), researchers from the U.S., Europe, Japan, and other countries tried different test-tube methods to predict the toxicity of 50 different chemicals such as aspirin, dioxin, diazepam (Valium), nicotine, Malathion, and lindane.

The effects of the chemical in humans were already known from poison control centers. The study's goal was to see how well the cellular tests matched actual human experience and to compare them with data previously reported for animal tests. The results were presented at the Conference of the Scandinavian Society for Cell Toxicology, in September 1996. The human cell tests were clearly superior. The rat LD50 tests--lethal dose tests that measure the dose of a chemical that kills 50% of the animals given it were only 59% accurate, and the mouse test were about 70% accurate. But the average human cell test was 77% accurate. Accuracy

Partisan Versus Partisan *Concluding Comments*

was boosted to 80% when the results from three different human cell tests were combined. The best combination was: A 24 hour exposure using Chang cells, developed by Lourdes Garza-Ocans of the University Autonoma De Nuevo Leon Mexico.

- A 24 hour exposure using HL-60 cells, developed by Noriho Tanaka of the Hatano food and drug safety center in Kanagawa Japan.

- A six week exposure using MRC-5 cells developed by Paul Dierick of the Institute for Hygience Epidemiology in Brussels Belgium.

The MEIC researchers have enlarged the number of chemicals they are testing. They are also using human cell tests to assess more complex processes, such as how drugs pass from the digestive tract into the bloodstream or from the blood into the brain, and to measure the toxicity of drug breakdown products. Some companies have used animals for these purposes but often get unreliable results, in addition to the ethical questions such tests raise. Some human cell tests are already well established. For example, the Eyetex system by Virginia C. Gordon and her colleagues (In Vitro International 16632 Millikan Ave., Irvine Ca. 92714) replaces the infamous Draize test, which assess the damage done as chemicals are dripped into the eyes of rabbits. An Eyetex vial contains proteins that turn cloudy in response to irritating chemicals, just as the cornea of the eye does. The test is faster and cheaper than the Draize test and is highly accurate, with a 98% predictive value.

NEW MEDICINES WITHOUT ANIMAL TESTS.

Pharmagene Laboratories, based in Royston England, is the first company to conduct new drug development and testing using human tissue and sophisticated technologies exclusively. With tools from molecular biology, biochemistry and analytical pharmacology, Pharmagene conducts extensive studies of human genes and investigates how drugs affect the actions of these genes or the proteins they make. While some have used animal tissues for this purpose, Pharmagene scientists believe that the discovery process is much more efficient with human tissues.

Pharmagene personnel came from large pharmaceutical companies, particularly Glaxo Welcome, Smith kline Beecham, Shire Pharmaceuticals and others. The company works on contract with other pharmaceutical companies.

It seems that Paul Silber's dogmatic claim that "we would not have in this century anything to replace the LD50 toxicity test," was a misjudgement, an error tantamount to the sanction of unabated demonic torture of millions of animals, under the aegis of necessity! And, Ender's position on AIDS doesn't seem to be tenable. Can it be true that a world without animals to vivisect could not learn to save people from AIDS, and from other dreadful diseases? That hardly seems probable, but is conceivable, which in no way alters the fact that animals should not be tyrannized. If justice is to prevail against prejudice, that factor weighed against the ongoing misery, pain, and death implicit in Ender's speculative opinion calls for a verdict against the continuation of vivisection as practiced.

Among the many causal factors underlying partisan attitudes in our Judeo-Christian culture is the conviction that human beings are intellectually and morally superior to animals and have a moral or divine right to exploit them as deemed necessary in the pursuit of self interest. Thus, ipso facto cruel sacrificial rituals become an acceptable norm.

Unnoticed is that the decisions to perform such bloody rituals, whether performed by religious sects, primitive cultures, or erudite professionals, are not logically derivable from religious beliefs, true or false beliefs of mental or moral inferiority, or empirical data.

Furthermore, if inferior mental and moral attributes were valid criteria for brutal exploitation, humans in various stages of mental retardation, psychosis, and depravity could be prime candidates for vivisection. But they are not prime candidates because they are **sentient** human beings. Animals, which are also **sentient** beings, have qualified for vivisection because they are not human, and are physiologically analogous to humans, making them not ideal, but acceptable analogues. An odious causal factor here is the evil of prejudice manifest in the "they are only animals" rationale: the results of which comprise a hell on earth for animals, sanctioned by partisan rhetoric and public apathy.

No assault of loaded questions, assumptions, false dilemmas, or past or predicted benefits, can override the fact that animals as well as humans have an inviolate property in themselves, which humans have no moral right to. I believe this dormant truism will eventually produce a change without precedent, as people free themselves from habitually and immorally perceiving animals as exploitable, disposable human property.

7

Honest criticism and sensitive appreciation are directed
not upon the poet but upon the poetry.
T. S. Eliot

The targets of "honest criticism" in the next six sections
are beliefs only, not the "poet." Thus the objective of
honest criticism will be served without disclosing identities,
by recourse to pseudo names.

On the Wearing of Fur

The incoherent "facts on wearing furs," by accountant Joan partisan, seems to be a self- refuting jumble. Which Joan can we believe? The Joan who defines herself as an abominable, bloodthirsty, and hard hearted creature, capable of any torture to animals. Or the Joan who wishes that an animal did not have to suffer and die so that she could have a fur coat. Partisans also have a wish. They wish that as many as forty animals and their orphaned babies did not have to suffer and die so that Joan could indulge and humor herself.

On The Wearing of Fur

Is it true that her fur coat is absolutely "necessary"? That state of affairs can be other than it is. According to an article by Greta Nilsson in the book "*Facts about Furs*," the synthetic product is in many ways superior to fur. It is impervious to moths, less costly, easier to maintain, and is as warm or warmer than fur. Evidence of the superior warmth and wind resistance of synthetic materials was the use by expeditions to Antarctica and Mt. Everest in the 1950s, of nylon furleen clothing in preference to fur garments.

Down-filled, and padded nylon parkas were, and may still be, the lightest and most waterproof protection available for frigid temperatures. However down plucking is cruel, thus down is an unacceptable product.

"The feet," says Dr. Loretta Smith, "are the last area of the body to get your circulating blood supply." Joan did not say that she wears fur-lined mukluks at "20 degrees below zero," so we can presume that she wore shoes and protective boots, and she felt like "the whole of me was in a sauna."

If animal fur is a necessity, should it not be so at 20 degrees below zero for the coldest part of the body, the lady's feet? if that is the coldest part of her body. This person's demeanor betrays an insensitivity to the suffering her conduct entails to her fellow creatures, whom she has deprived of both fur coats and life.

On The Wearing of Fur

Mr. Joel partisan of Cork furriers is "satisfied" with "the morality of selling natural fur." He claimed that the fake furs made from synthetic-based products, entail more harm to the environment than natural fur. Real people, he believes, don't wear fake fur.

Were we to be conquered by a race of super beings from space who took a fancy to our hides as wearing apparel, would Joel acquiesce to the morality of commerce in human skin and hair? Or would he, astute man that he is, strenuously object and demonstrate against the fashionable use of human skin and hair?

Interest speaks all languages and acts all parts, but Joel the ecologist is also in error.

It is a little known but ominous fact that animal husbandry and fur farming are today a great source of pollution to our good earth. Can anyone be justified in causing preventable suffering and death to either man or beast and fouling the collective nest?

"Real people don't wear fake fur," is meaningless nonsense, in defense of the indefensible. It's because real people wear natural fur that real live animals-many live animals-have suffered, and do suffer and die.

On The Wearing of Fur

The fur industry advertisement in the newspaper failed to deliver what it promised: talking truth. Finding themselves unable to cope with charges that are difficult if not impossible to refute, the Associated Fur Industries of Chicagoland attempted to show that the animal advocates (Partisans) are guilty of misconduct.

This is a diversion that can be very effective in controversy since it serves to deflect attention from the main issue, and tends to gain support for the accused party. With just a few well chosen, emotion-laden words, a very humane and compassionate outlook is characterized as "...an issue of individual rights." These are inappropriate but powerful symbols. It is not the legal right to wear fur that is at issue. The issue is wrongfulness based on the cruelty, suffering, and death entailed in the wearing of fur.

Intuit the truth! urges talk truth, don't underestimate the comfort and pleasure of a new fur coat. Is this sound advice and truth that can be justified in light of the relevant facts?

Fur coats consist of the skin and fur of animals which were either raised or trapped and killed. Estimates have gone as high as three animals caught and discarded to get the fourth one the trapper finds suitable for market. When the steel jaw trap snaps shut on an animal's leg, the animal will thrash about in pain, panic, and terror, sometimes breaking teeth on the trap to no avail. And sometimes the victim will succeed in achieving freedom after much struggle, by leaving a foot in the trap. The majority of animals are trapped on land, and eventually exhausted by their struggle, and lie quietly without food or water until the trapper returns perhaps several days later. If the animal has not died it must be killed, which may be done by strangulation, clubbing, or stomping. Animals that are trapped in water invariably drown. Trapping

On The Wearing of Fur

regulations that have not prevented the decimation of huge animal populations to near extinction, are a tragic sham.

The fur farm horror, is another fur industry closet truth. An energetic animal such as a fox or mink, suffers horribly in the tiny jail in which it spends its life. Neurotic behavior and self mutilation is common among "ranched" fur animals.

Summer brings another hell to "ranched" animals in sultry areas. Those with thick fur cannot perspire, as can some animals without thick fur. Thus they are subject to heat stress and lie suffering in their tiny cages. In temperate climes, the onset of winter brings the animals to their final torture, a violent death, probably by electrocution, for which a clamp is applied to the mouth and an electrode inserted in the anus. Some manage to escape their electrocution by dying from protracted suffering. Some lose their tongues, which have stuck frozen to the cage floor.

These are the verifiable facts, which don't sell newspapers or fur coats but haunt Partisans. These facts haunt Partisans because of man's cruelty to animals, and what people will do, and say out of self-interest. Contrary to what the fur people would have us believe, a fake fur coat takes less energy to produce than a real fur coat. According to G.H. Smith, Resident Engineer, Scientific Research Laboratory at Ford Motor Company, the Btu's to produce fake, trapped, and ranched furs are, respectively 120,300, 433,000 and 7,965,800! On a finite planet of limited resources, the Btu factor-aside from the hellish cruelty-should be ample justification for an end to the bloody fur industry.

68

On The Wearing of Fur

My critique of the fur mongers was predicated in part upon the research and testimony of G.H. Smith, Resident Engineer, Scientific Research Laboratory, Ford Motor Company, and the work of another engineer, William J.Sauber of the American Institute of Astronautics, author of *"The Fourth Kingdom."*

The response of Bud partisan of the retail fur industry seems to have been motivated by self-interest. Interest exerts a strong influence upon the conduct of people. They can become creatures of selective awareness, seeing in a situation what they wish to see, while passing over what they do not want to see. Thus an animal's skin, fur, and life becomes a "renewable resource," like a cabbage or tree. And an industry that brutally raises, traps, and skins sometimes alive millions of animals, (303,087,965 world wide in 1977-78,) is alleged to be one of America's strongest supporters of animal welfare and ecology.

It's true as Bud claims, that people are often ignorant of the facts before taking a stand. A fact that Bud is either ignorant of, or has chosen to ignore, is that we can make fifteen fake fur coats with the resources required to make one natural fur garment. For many people it is still impossible to serve God and Mammon- "for where your treasure is, there will your heart be also."

It's true as Bud asserts, that fake fur is not biodegradable. A good warm cloth coat made from the wool of sheep humanely shorn, is biodegradable, and is a benign alternative.

8

Shelters

Fay partisan's article, "Shelters", warrants criticism because error can be misleading when conjoined with truth. Fay's concern-battered women, and children-unable to find even temporary shelter and help, is a frightful thing to contemplate. The answer would seem to be more facilities as soon as possible. This is the truth implicit in her article.

Fay's first partisan question: "Are animals more important than children?" is followed by: "Why is there much more money available for animal shelters than human shelters; does this disparity reflect society's priorities?"

Society's priorities, broadly described, are immutable, the same today as yesterday, and what they will be tomorrow:

Shelters

They can be summarized as whatever is believed to be in the best interest of society, which doesn't always correspond with the truth of the matter. To intimate as Fay has, that society may place a greater value on animals than people, betrays either ignorance of the germane facts or malevolence towards animals. Or, as is often the case, a mixture of ignorance and malevolence. If we were to use her money criterion to determine society's priorities, we would be no less mistaken than she is. The money spent on non-essentials, such as cigarettes, alcohol, gambling, drugs, status symbols, and a plethora of soon discarded gadgets, does not reflect society's indifference to human victims of violence.

One wonders if Fay is aware of what animal shelters do, and what they entail in terms of compassion, kindness, and the saving of life. Would she have us do away with the "no-kill shelters" that feed and mend sick and broken bodies, and often find loving homes for animals? Or would she have us do away with the facilities that kill so very many unwanted and homeless dogs and cats annually, the inevitable result of a universal quasi-aristocratic attitude in regard to animals? Ramifications of that attitude can't be eliminated from the realm of sentience but can be controlled in the human condition, as exemplified by the abolition of slavery.

The women's question: "Are animals really more important than women and children?" can be best answered with another question: Are animals more important than women, and children to a society that brutally kills several billion animals annually?

The slaughterhouses, and killing of abandoned, homeless, and unwanted animals will continue as long as animals are unjustifiably classified as human property. The no-kill shelter and "fixing of animals" is a palliative, but not a cure.

The need for change, whether it be in the interest of

Shelters

people or animals, will eventually be fulfilled, I believe, but it must first be known to exist. Calling attention to the need is a step in the right direction. But articles such as Fay's must not be swallowed whole to the detriment of other realities, such as the unceasing injustice suffered by animals, whose only hope is concerned Partisans working for change.

9

Whales

The short article about alleged Soviet folly by Tom partisan is of ominous significance.

He didn't need a book, just a few words to exemplify the essence of parochialism. "Am I my brothers keeper" is the battle cry of the quintessential partisan, unwittingly opposed to the moral progress of the universe.

Whales

The effort to "help a couple of dumb whales" survive a trap into which they ventured, was a project motivated, I think, by kindly feeling for animals in great distress. In an ideal world there would be a dearth of cruelty, and an abundance of kindly feeling.

Every act of kindness is a micro-step in that direction. Thus the value, meaning, and importance of the "whaling" effort is significant in terms of the implicit morality of the attempt to save the whales' lives. That the Soviets may not have been motivated by kindly feeling is a possibility with which we need not be concerned.

It's the deed only that can be seen and known from our vantage point. And deeds determine us, as we determine them.

Whales

As soon as we abandon our own reason and rely on the reason of others, there may be no end to the ensuing harm. The newspaper editorial about saving the whales provides a cogent example.

The argument that only in a perfect world could the romantic notion of freedom for animals as well as for men be a reality, is counter factual. The fault lies in the silly assumption that a perfect world is a necessary condition for animal or human freedom.

It is in our imperfect world that progressive sociopolitical and a modicum of humane legislation has passed, imperfection notwithstanding. And it is in our imperfect world that this writer claimed that ideas of wild animals being forever free was romanticism. It is in the same world that the same person informed a few million people that: If even but a fraction of the many people expected annually to see the captive whales materialize, it will help the whales more than an army of protesters and demonstrators.

We have here a textbook example of theory contradicting experience.

The relevant facts tell a different story. Thousands of animals were confined to zoos and ogled by many millions of curious and interested people. Some of those animals have suffered severe decimation, attributable to human predation, which tends to refute this author's exposure thesis. Only under exceptional circumstances can we help animals by locking them up. To arbitrarily put an animal behind bars or glass is to say: This creature is only an animal, and only a means to human ends.

A perfect world is impossible in a world of imperfect people, but in the measure that we refuse to harm our fellow creatures, human or nonhuman, we have a less imperfect world. And in the measure that we incarcerate our fellow crea-

Whales

tures for our amusement, or profit we have a less perfect world.

10

Animal Rights

In common speech, words like justice, rights, and freedom can have ambiguous interpretations and are often the cause of acrimonious debate.

Acrimonious, perhaps, because of an element of antipathy, resulting in distortion, and error. Mary partisan's article is a typical example. "Animals can't have rights," she says "because they lack the necessary intelligence. " It is upon this premise, and through reductio ad absurdum arguments, i.e., by showing what silly consequences "rights" would have, that she takes her stand against animals.

Animal Rights

Philosopher David Hume did not concur. "Next to the ridicule of denying an evident truth is that of taking much pain to defend it, and no truth appears to me more evident than that beasts are endowed with thought and reason as well as men."

We know from experience that animals remember past events, anticipate events in the future, and exhibit emotions; that some animals, i.e., nonhuman primates and some birds, can communicate with humans as well as with members of their own species.

If by "rights" Mary means the civil rights established by the 13th and 14th amendments to the American constitution she has an irrefutable argument. If she means, however, that animals do not have the right to be free of human tyranny, she holds a widely held opinion-an opinion that is the reason this book was written.

There are many tens of thousands of Partisans about whom I will not generalize beyond saying: They are by and large opposed to any form of cruelty, whether it be to animals or humans. To imply, as Mary does, that even a tiny fraction of such people believe that it would be wrong to save a dying child from an infection, or that plants should have the same rights as animals, is an attempt to make a kindly humane position appear to be absurd.

That position, as I understand it, entails an overarching interest in compassion, kindness, and justice for animals. To conclude, as Pearl does, that that would militate against saving a dying person from infection is nonsensical. In a world of Partisan moral concern, life threatening bacteria or viruses would be as subject to liquidation, I believe, as a psychopathic killer on the prowl.

Would we, Mary asks, also have to in some way prevent some animals from killing other animals? I do believe that we are morally obliged to prevent needless animal suffering that is practicable to prevent, without creating as much or more suffering. It would not cause more suffering to abolish cock, dog, or bull fighting or to bell the cat, but it would cause more suffering to bell the tiger because tigers are not constituted to eat grass.

It is folly to pursue ends for which there are no means, and a predator-free world is one such end. On the other hand, a world in which cruel human predation upon animals in its innumerable forms is minimized, is an end for which there are means: namely the huge Partisan contingent vehemently opposed to any and all forms of cruel human predation. And that probably makes it attainable.

Animal Rights

Hal partisan's critique of animal advocates (Partisans) as described by John Pivodich, is one more bit of nonsense for the archives of cant.

"How," he asks, "can animals have rights?" He insists that they can't because they are "instinctual," as opposed to "ethical beings" such as humans.

Hal's premise is a redundant staple in the book of partisan error, authorizing, he apparently believes, the moral right to tyrannize animals with impunity. Contrary to his distinction between "mice and men," animals don't have a monopoly on instinct, and people don't have a monopoly on ethics, broadly defined.

But contrary to the parochial world view, animals have moral rights. An animal's moral rights derive from its right to exist. If, say, a raccoon is caught in a trap, the animal has a moral right to escape. That the racoon has a moral right to escape can be known independently of experience, if one is rational and objective by putting one's self in the animal's position. To argue as one trapper did, that the animal has no right to escape his trap, is tantamount to claiming that the animal has no moral right to preserve its life, which is prima facie nonsense.

Paradoxically, an animal's moral right to preserve its life doesn't save it from the butcher, the hunter, the trapper, the furrier, vivisector, wholesale euthanasia, or from other animals. And to cite the obvious, the moral or natural right of humans to exist is a human concept beyond the ken of animals, domestic or wild, and many human "ethical beings."

I would have to agree with Hal if he had argued that animals cannot have the same civil rights as humans, which seems to be obvious. What is not obvious to the Hals of our world, is that animals should have the right to live and not be tyrannized by humans, which as human property they don't have.

Animal Rights

Emancipation can only happen if made to happen by the ascendence of biocentrism, which will entail a great struggle. "You forget," said the devil, "I, too, have been evolving."

Given the penchant for aggression, murder, and rape that so many of we "ethical" two-legged saints exhibit, it's bitterly absurd that Hal should cite an ethical sense, as justification to deprive animals of rights.

11

It Upsets Them

The writer's article was a typical example of partisan insensitivity. "Wool," wrote Mr. journalist, "Sorry, sheep are sometimes injured to get it, and the experience upsets them." "Upsets them?" Most of all wool used in clothing comes from Australia, where about 158 million sheep are raised for wool before being slaughtered. During cold weather, hundreds of thousands die after late shearing because a closely shorn sheep is very sensitive to cold.

Another barbarism that "upsets them" is mulesing, which entails having huge sections of the sheep's back (skin not wool) sliced off with shears. No anesthesia is used. The exposed tissue when it heals, scars up, pulling the skin tight. This prevents moisture from collecting in the wrinkled skin of Merino sheep, and prevents insects from laying their eggs in the folds.

It Upsets Them

During the painful healing process, the tyrannized animal lies still in the field for days, or takes tiny steps, and falls, and tries again and falls over again and again. Some farms have computer controlled shearing machinery that holds the terrified sheep's face in a clamp while a sensor directs the instrument which, does not always sense teats, or other tissue before the cutter reaches them.

Apparently Mr. Journalist doesn't care what we do to animals, which would explain why he writes as he does. Contrary to what he writes, the crusade for animals does not seek to elevate animals to a human moral plane. No, Mr. Journalist, there will not be universal suffrage for animals. What there will be, I believe, is an end one day to the most enduring demonic tyranny in the history of our planet.

12

On Hunting

I remember it very well. I had never aimed my rifle at any living thing, but I jumped at the opportunity to go hunting rabbits in southern Illinois. My father had never hunted either, and also jumped. Off we went in an over-populated sedan, loaded with sandwiches artillery, and in high mental spirits, intensified by strong liquor. The following sun-shy morning found us plodding along in a cold, damp, seemingly lifeless forest, and I harbored a secret. If I saw a rabbit, I wouldn't shoot it.

On Hunting

We did not see any rabbits. As all good, not so good, and bad things must come to an end, our great safari was on its last mile sans stars and moon but with one hunter's resolve to never jump again.

And then it happened! Something above (which could not have been a rabbit) made a scary sound, which was immediately followed by a round of artillery that caused a thump of something hitting the ground: a huge harmless owl. At the time I did not have the feeling of revulsion which I do in retrospect. I learned something about hunting not to be found in *Field and Stream*.

I have not jumped since that educational night in the Centralia, Illinois woods, but was subsequently exposed to the opinions of various hunters, one of whom I have christened Sam Flinton. Sam apparently seeking approval, informed me that there were "intelligent, urbane, and skillful hunters," that participate in a "moral, legal sport," not only to put food on the table, but to forge "character." The source of these edifying words acknowledged the existence of "slob hunters," whose conduct tends to vitiate the image of the "ethical hunter." He also alluded to the management of game and conservation, as being the business of sportsmanship and the hunt morality.

Flinton's attempt to distinguish between the "honest, ethical hunter," and the "slob hunter," was a determined but futile effort to sustain an untenable position. Drawing attention to the fact that what is true of a part is not necessarily true of the whole does not rule out the fact that the results-the tyranny of animals-is produced by the whole.

Terms such as moral, honest, ethical, legal, and sportsmanship, are calculated to define and justify a breed apart involved in an honorable character-molding activity. Whether or not such terms are applicable must be deter-

On Hunting

mined by hunting's consequences, such as violent death and suffering that may be caused by a lingering infected wound. A less than exhaustive account of consequences must include the "slob hunter" who is by definition a hunter responsible for:

- Bear hunting with dogs, a double-edged act of cruelty.
- The killing of wolves to ensure an ample supply of game for human hunters.
- Pigeon shoots which entail frequent ritualistic decapitation.
- Providing dogs with small animals to tear apart.
- The use of bow and arrow which, can entail multiple wounds, infections and slow painful death.
- Killing farmers' horses and cows.
- Defiance of "no trespassing" signs; cutting fences and gates.
- Taking "pot shots" at "no hunting" signs.
- Hunting from aircraft, snowmobiles, dune buggies, or swamp buggies.
- Hunting while drunk and careless.
- Hunting out of season and exceeding bag limit.
- Shooting endangered species and song birds.
- Shooting several animals in order to get one "impressive" trophy.
- Threatening farmers or police who try to restrain them.
- Accidental human slaughter.
- Leaving the land strewn with rotting animals.
- Participating in "canned" hunting: killing animals in an enclosure from which they cannot escape.

The following article appeared in the informative newspaper "ANIMAL PEOPLE" March, 1993.

The 1992-93 hunting season closed with a spate of killings by hunters apparently desperate to shoot anything. Victims include trumpeter swans,

On Hunting

shotgunned January 1 on the Winterthur Museum Grounds in Wilmington, Delaware; a tame deer at the St Clare County humane society in Port Huron, Michigan January 4; cows killed in Clay County, Missouri, between Christmas and New Year's Day; and three dairy cows killed near Warsaw, Ohio, on January 16. Michael Adamson, 20, of Barberton, Ohio and a 17-year-old companion face charges in the latter case. Ronald Smith and his infant daughter escaped injury December 30 when hunters trying to jacklight rabbits--after midnight--sprayed the baby's bedroom with gunfire. Charles W. Tipton, 44, of Lorain, Ohio, was charged in the incident. Ohio ended the hunting season with only 66 game wardens on duty, down from a quota of 88 (one per county.)

Judging by the consequences of the hunting enterprise: the claim of morality, and the attempt to substantiate the claim by the distinction made between the ethical hunter and the slob hunter are examples of muddle-headedness. The self styled "ethical" hunter no less than the "slob" hunter brutalize animals. Not with the tyrant's plea of necessity, but with the plea of misleading language in a vain attempt to justify human violence, and the suffering and death of animals.

13

The Need to Know

"The more extensive a mans knowledge of what has been done,
the greater will be his power of knowing what to do."
Disraeli

I knew what I had to do when I discovered what others were doing to animals, which I believe should be a matter of universal concern and remedial action. The examples outlined on the following pages are not after the fact realities, inasmuch as they keep happening again and again.

The Need to Know

The many ways or times the world of humans has tyrannized animals is unknowable. But it can't be denied that everyone has a right to know what can be known, if they are so inclined: a right to which the mass media is either oblivious or not concerned to publicize often, if at all. Thus there is a need to know, as well as a right to know, and this book would be very incomplete sans some germane examples of what animals have endured and are suffering because of human tyranny.

* Indicates source

*1 Aounde, Cameroon Having seized an infant gorilla, hunter Ntsama Ondo came close to his short-lived dream of affluence. But the infant's huge family would not be tyrannized. About 60 gorillas marched into town and demonstrated in silent protest, to no avail. They were not silent when they returned the next night.

They pounded on homes, whereupon the village chief demanded that the infant be returned. After which the troop peacefully returned to their forest, as reported by L' Action.

*2...Meanwhile, free living gorillas every bit as gentle and intelligent as Koko and Binta are quietly being eaten into extinction in parts of their African habitat. Yes, eaten! The commercialized illegal killing of gorillas and other primates for "bush meat" has reached truly alarming levels. Yet this very important news is tragically under-reported.

*3 "Buddy," a yellow lab, was killed horribly in a cross-country ski area. The trap was baited with chicken parts and Buddy put his head into the trap, setting it off. His owner was unable to release the trap, and finally when a friend was able to, Buddy died painfully in his arms.

The Need to Know

*3 Here is an excerpt from Jill's report about the death-row dogs of Taiwan. One dog had a broken leg, another an open, seeping wound on his side...many had pus filled eyes. A puppy lay dead in the last holding pen; other; older dogs lay in wasted condition, close to death. The healthier ones walked towards us trustingly, begging for release with pleading eyes. The cages were covered with so much urine and feces that the dogs slipped on the floor. A mother dog was desperately trying to feed two puppies in the filth...In the worst facility, the animals were sickly and trembling with fright. When our investigators arrived, workers were filling up a concrete tank with water. Overhead a hook and pulley were attached to a stainless steel cage waiting to be filled with dogs for drowning...

*1 As reported by the Sea Shepherd Conservation Society, the floes of the Gulf of St. Lawrence were the killing field for more than 500,000 harp seals in 1998. The seals, claim the Canadian government, eat too many cod. Entrepreneurs selling seal penis' for aphrodisiacs to gullible Asians would probably agree.

*5 Here are excerpts from a paper about the American Military's experiments(exclusive of grotesque details). More than half a million animals are used annually in intramural experiments conducted by the military, at a cost of almost 110 million dollars. These figures, however, are just the tip of the iceberg. Extramural research projects account for even larger costs.

Military experiments are often painful. Oversight is poor. Former research facility staff members and veterinarians cite poor animal care and neglect at military facilities. Military experiments are as grim as animal experiments can

The Need to Know

get. Many doctors and former researchers have identified experiments that are irrelevant to solving real human problems and that in some instances create new problems, in addition to wasting valuable resources. Burn experiments, which are grotesquely cruel and scientifically useless, have been conducted at the Naval Weapons Center in China Lake, California...

*6 Russians flock to Beijing, China, to buy fur coats of mink, rabbit, goat and dog. On Chawaowai Street, the center of a busy area known as the Russian Market, more than 100 stalls line the alley selling racks and racks of coats. Almost all will end up in Russia. Trade between the two countries has nearly doubled since 1990, to 6.8 billion.

"The quality is not very good but, it's cheap," said a Russian trader. Chinese workers earn less than $100 a month to sew the furs, making coats very cheap. One shopkeeper says he sells 10,000 fur coats a year. Some of the mink pelts are imported from the United States. The dog furs, though, all come from China. The dogs are raised on farms: their fur is raised for coats and meat for food. "It's just like a poultry farm," says Zhuang De Yu, a merchant on Chaowai Street. As long as there is a market this will continue. Business is booming in Beijing's free market. Everyone is to busy making money to worry about animals.

*7 It's one of the largest livestock markets in America, shipping approximately one million animals every year, and is allegedly one of the largest animal abusers in America. Becky Sandstedt tearfully investigated conditions there for over a year. Conditions such as: a downed cow, emaciated and near death, dragged by a chain tied around her leg. As her body scraped the ground, she cried and struggled to escape, her

The Need to Know

cries were ignored; after all she was "only an animal." Conditions such as: Several downed pigs left in a pen without food or water, one dead and the rest dying. When the slaughter truck arrived, the injured and weak pigs were beaten and shocked to make them drag themselves onto the truck. One pig that could not make it was grabbed by an ear and dragged up the ramp into the truck.

Conditions such as: The brutal treatment of a downed calf, probably a week or two old, in a walkway. The calf could have been humanely moved. But beating and kicking was the routine method for a calf too weak to get up, so the animal was just left there to die.

These were not infrequent brutalities. They were everyday occurrences at a place littered with the dead, the dying, and the tyrannized, because they were "only animals."

*8 The starving dog drank out of a dirty puddle near the stake he was tied to. But the puddle dried up, leaving the emaciated animal with neither food nor water. By the time a neighbor called the ASPCA, the poor dog was too weak to bark, or stand up, and every rib could be seen on his dehydrated body.

When the dog was brought to Bergh Memorial Hospital, he weighed 45 pounds, less than half what a dog his size should weigh. He had a number of infections brought on by malnutrition and weakness, but he did survive. When questioned, the owner said he was trying to starve his dog to death!

*8 It's probably happening at this moment, as it probably has been happening and will keep happening until universally prohibited. The little animal, maybe a fox, or coyote, or wolf, wearing a fur coat that a human animal wants to wear, makes a bad move. The steel jaws don't care who it is; they snap

The Need to Know

shut on living fur, bone, and flesh. He or she snaps back, breaking precious teeth; she pulls, struggles, but the steel jaws that were made to hold, hold fast. She has babies to feed back at her den, babies that will starve without their mother! And it all keeps happening again, and again, and again.

*9 The painful, brutal abuse of horses is commonplace in America today. An articulate Tennessee walking horse might describe the suffering he endures as a result of a soring process that makes each step painful, and forces him into the unnatural high-stepping gait, that horse show judges and audiences applaud.

...Soring a horse's front hoof and forelegs can be accomplished a number of ways. Heavy chains are used during training to produce an exaggerated high stepping gait. Nails are driven into the tender sole of a horses hoof, or the hoof wall is cut to the quick.

Chemical irritants such as diesel fuel, kerosene, or mustard oil are rubbed on the low forelegs in pursuit of blue ribbons or a smoother ride.

Many thoroughbred race horses are injected with pain-masking drugs, steroids, and/or other dangerous substances to enable them to run while injured or to enhance their performance.

The cost to the animal can be painful cartilage and tendon deterioration. Some crippled horses end up at the slaughterhouse, where they may arrive in worse condition because they are routinely crammed into double deck trailers designed for smaller animals. A twelve hour trip without water can lead to gouged eyes, broken bones, and other untreated injuries.

Polluted, paved, and heavy traffic urban areas are no place for a carriage horse. Bearing heavy loads, breathing exhaust fumes and being hit by cars and trucks are only the most obvious problems and dangers they must endure.

Many carriage horses are older animals that are not physically fit to haul people around under any circumstances and certainly not on congested city streets.

*10 They are called puppy mills because they breed puppies by the thousands, which is lucrative. They are by and large unscrupulous breeders without regard for the interest of the animals. Congenital defects such as deafness, epilepsy, hip dysplasia, and behavioral problems may be attributed to puppy-mill breeding. The mills sell their pathetic victims to pet shops, that in turn foist them on fleeceable customers, not yet aware that a shelter is a better alternative.

*10 To put as many as five egg-laying chickens into a one-square-foot cage where they will spend the rest of their lives is to brutalize them. The same may said about the new-born male chicks that are discarded in plastic bags where most suffocate before being ground up for chick feed and fertilizer.

The same may be said about female pigs that are bred constantly. They must be strapped to the floor of their tiny cages during birth and while nursing, if they are not to crush their babies.

The same charge of brutality is applicable to the cruel practice of making cows into milk machines by keeping them pregnant. And, tyranny is the appropriate charge for the trauma of both mother and baby that is taken from its mother to become (depending on gender) either veal chops or another tyrannized cow, ad infinitum.

*11 The Sri Lankans dispatch dolphins by harpooning, spearing, drowning, hacking, shooting, and other violent methods.

The Need to Know

It was estimated in the early 1990s that 62,000 dolphins were killed each year by a combination of netting and harpooning.

*12 It was in the 1960s that the Association for Biomedical Research touted the "sophistication" of dissecting higher animals. Thus the subsequent dissection of 100,000 cats annually symbolized sophistication without precedent. The chain of supply starts with the licensed animal broker that procures cats from various legal and illegal sources such as animal shelters and "free to good home ads." A group in Mexico paid children $1 for each cat brought in, which were then drowned and shipped to America. An undercover investigation of a large biological supply company revealed that they were obtaining live cats and then embalming them, often while the cats were still alive.

*13 The investigation at a fur farm revealed a farmer killing foxes by anal execution, a slow and painful method denounced by the American Veterinary Medical Association. They found animals with painful untreated injuries that were exposed to ice and snow. They also witnessed live chickens used to feed the foxes being forced feet first into a grinder.

*14 It was in China that David Usher allegedly witnessed a defanged lioness mauling cows, sheep, goats, chickens, and other farm animals to death. He described it as a gruesome, earthshaking, noisy torture, in which cows often took over an hour to stop shrieking and struggling.

Two or more dogs were brought into the cage on leashes, taunted by trainers until they were furious, and then unleashed to destroy each other.

Cockfights were to the death. Large dogs such as Alsatians and Labrador were put into a cage with a cow, whose tail was ripped off, legs grossly maimed, and ears ripped off and shredded. Large dogs were similarly used to kill small goats and chickens.

This happened in a theme park in Chendu, owned by Huaxin corporation, a multinational based in Singapore.

*15 The kitten had wandered into a university building looking for warmth against the cold air. Unfortunately the building was Tolman Hall, headquarters of UC Berkley Professor Jonathan Doe. Twenty-four hours later the kitten would be dead, her body drained of blood, her brain dissected. Isolated instance?

In this very same building a monkey had lain for weeks in excruciating pain, slowly dying from gangrene and neglect... death being the only solution to its terrible pain and suffering. The veterinarian who put this poor animal out of his misery later wrote to Professor Doe:

"...it was necessary today to euthanize one of your primates. I do not make a practice of euthanizing research animals without the concurrence of the investigator, but in this case, the necessity was obvious... The perineal area and the entire scrotum were necrotic and gangrenous with full thickened skin death. The feet and ears were also involved. The animal was in such discomfort that he could not climb to his lixit to drink and was observed by the animal technician and myself attempting to drink his own urine..."

Another isolated incident?

For years, students and veterinarians have documented instances of tiny kittens screaming with pain from inadequate anesthesia, of dirty surgery, filthy conditions, and neglect of unbelievable proportions. They have told of the refusal of Professor Doe and his staff to follow recommendations of veterinarians and federal agencies, even going so far as to

The Need to Know

prevent veterinarians from treating sick and suffering animals. Uncensored University documents revealed autopsy reports on animals that died in Doe's laboratory. The reports revealed a continuing pattern of animal suffering, negligence and abuse: Sick and suffering animals, paralyzed and experimented on for days at a time. Monkeys and cats dying of brain infections. Some of the animals were so weak, they never recovered from surgery. Others were simply found dead in their cages.

In his basement laboratory, monkeys and cats have stereotaxic devices screwed and bolted into their heads, portions of their skulls removed, and electrodes inserted into their brains for up to 100 hours at a time. All this was taking place to determine how humans perceive color!

*15 For years, the cold and impenetrable walls of the Letterman Army Institute reverberated with the screams of suffering animals. Dogs, cats, monkeys, pigs, sheep, rabbits, and mice were brutalized day after day, in excruciatingly painful biological, chemical, and nuclear warfare experimentation.

J.P. Novic, formerly a member of the over sight committee at the Letterman Army Institute of Research, relived her own painful experiences: "The treatment of animals was absolutely despicable...the suffering was immense. Primates were housed in cages so small they could barely stand up. Most had become psychotic...some banging their heads on the cages...others crouched in a corner, head in hand." She finished her recollections with a heartfelt plea, "please do not allow UC San Francisco to go in there and continue the horror."

*1 Hidden cameras have caught live animal vendors at Asian style markets countless times in atrocities-not just in San Fran-

The Need to Know

cisco, where the markets are a heated public issue, but in virtually every U.S. and Canadian city with a Chinatown. Frogs are typically piled in large containers or confined in wire cages without food or water. Turtles have been seen having their shells sliced from their bodies while fully alive and being hacked and pounded repeatedly with dull knives before being decapitated. At one market, an investigator found a turtle still moving with carapace cut open and its internal organs displayed in full view of the shoppers.

Many animals, including birds and mammals, are boiled to death, in the belief that adrenaline released by pain and fear enhances the flavor and medicinal value of the flesh, especially for men.

*16 In East Bernard, Texas, members of a local high school baseball team brutally tortured and killed Tiger, a cat, because he defecated on the baseball diamond; in Barstow, Florida, two boys hung and dismembered a dog with a weed eater; and in Hamilton, Tennessee, three boys shot and killed a neighborhood dog by repeatedly shooting BBs into his mouth. Reports to The Animal Legal Defense Fund cruelty line indicate that crimes against animals are occurring every day, in all areas of the country.

*3 Kiev, Ukraine. Investigators at the Budka death factory heard animal screams outside the gates and discovered that 20,000 stray cats and dogs a year were being snatched from the streets, brutally killed and skinned for leather.
(That Budka factory was shut down).
    In China, government-approved dog beating squads round up pets from the streets and cats are drowned in boiling water to be cooked for dinner.

The Need to Know

*15 UC San Francisco. In vision "research" vivisectors surgically implant monkeys with eye coils and head implants, before inserting electrodes into their brains. The eyes of kittens are punctured with hypodermic needles, their brains with electrodes. The brains of cats are destroyed through the use of electrical currents.

The eyes of kittens are stitched shut before inserting electrodes into their brains. They are killed several weeks later. In hearing research, this vivisector destroys portions of the brains of cats using "sharpened watchmaker's forceps." She then inserts electrodes into the brains, allowing the cats to live 8 to 12 weeks before killing them.

In pain research, the spinal cords of monkeys are severed, allowing them to live 2 to 3 days before killing them to remove their brains.

*15 In impotence research, this vivisector tyrannizes dogs and monkeys to study penile erection by implanting compression devices (pumps) and electrodes inside their penises. Dogs that develop infections or acute urinary retention are immediately killed.

In studying how drugs affect penile erection, the abdomens of dogs are opened to implant probes before the dog's entire penis is denuded, which is followed by the placement of two 21-gauge needles in the organ.

*7 Inspired by the notorious California downers law, the new Colorado Law was designed to *allow* diseased and disabled animals to be sent to slaughter, regardless of their suffering. Whether or not such philistinism engendered the following behavior is an open question. The assault at the Turlock Livestock Auction (TLA) was brutal and mindless. Angered by

The Need to Know

visitors from Farm Sanctuary (FS), the manager of TLA mercilessly beat to death a critically ill calf who had the misfortune of being in the wrong place the wrong time. First the calf was beaten over the head with a stick. When it became apparent that he was still alive, the calf was beaten with a hammer. Following this, the calf suffered more minutes before dying.

*17 Kelly Tansy, a former Ringling Brothers performer, told his story to PAWS about the tyranny of the circus! Yes, tyranny! His first day with the circus included his baptism in cruelty. An elephant was being beaten so mercilessly and efficiently that she screamed! This sort of treatment, he soon learned, was the modus operandi, a necessary procedure. It was necessary, of course to lock up the chimps in small cages when they were not entertaining and to keep the elephants chained-as Tansy put it-continuously. It was even necessary to beat animals while they performed, for which   it was essential that the trainer have a weak demonic mind in a strong body. "It sure as hell is necessary to use the coercive power of electricity to train an elephant, and don't believe anybody that denies it." (This came from another trainer.) Tansy explained   that animals can't have anything near a decent life while on the road with the circus.

*13 In the United States alone, more than $45 million has been poured into sleep deprivation experiments since 1993. Millions more are spent around the world. Many of these experiments involve rats, primates, cats, mice, and rabbits, and despicable methods have been devised to keep these animals from satisfying their basic need to sleep. Cats, who normally nap on and off throughout a 24-hour period, are tied to moving treadmills and forced to walk to the point of collapse.

The Need to Know

Similar methods are used in other countries. Experimenters at the Universite Claude Bernard in France recently cemented electrodes to the skulls of cats and then forced them to keep afloat on narrow platforms in water drums for an agonizing 24 hours. At the University of Helsinki, experimenters kept 3-month old rats awake on tiny water platforms for three days! Adrian Morrison, at the University of Pennsylvania, has received more than $1 million for sleep deprivation experiments. In one experiment he suctioned out pieces of the cat's brain and then watched what happened when they weren't allowed to sleep. In other studies he electrically burned out portions of cat's brains, used plexiglass devices to keep them from shutting their eyelids, and crushed their spinal cords with jeweler's forceps.

*11 Mother and baby manatee were swimming calmly in a warm, shallow-water inlet between sessions of nursing. The mother fed along the bottom on sea grass, her favorite food. In the distance came the whine of a speed boat: teenagers on an outing, skimming along at 25 knots on a favorite Florida saltwater river. As the boat and its vicious spinning propeller drew close, the boys swerved to avoid a tall signpost in the middle of the river. The mother manatee also turned, swimming towards her calf. In an instant, the boat's bow bounced twice over submerged objects. The outboard engine however, jerked up two times in quick succession, its propeller and lower skag ripping across the backs of the unseen manatees below.

The calf was killed instantly as the deadly propeller blades cut the small animal nearly in half. The mother's fate was far more horrible. For what must have been an hour or more of pure torture, the mother manatee swam in shock as she bled from multiple gaping wounds. She finally died a few feet from her calf. Just twenty yards away, the sign on the post in the middle of the river read:

MANATEE AREA-IDLE SPEED.

*10 Greyhound racing is a form of entertainment which results in the slaughter of 30,000 greyhounds each year, according to the International Society for Animal Rights.

The carnage starts in the quest for fast animals, which requires that many animals are born so that a few with a money making potential materialize. A dog that doesn't qualify is destroyed: the fate, perhaps, of fifty percent of all puppies. Those allowed to live must be trained and are introduced to "blooding." Cats, kittens, chickens, and rabbits are a living incentive to coax greyhounds to run faster. The helpless terrified live lures are torn to pieces by the greyhounds. Painful injuries are very common and endured by many dogs as long as they race. They are also drugged, beaten, and starved by their human owners to make them run faster.

When they fail to perform as expected they are cast aside and replaced. Thousands of greyhounds are shot, abandoned, left to starve and dehydrate, electrocuted, beaten to death, and sold to vivisection laboratories. Their crime? They are "only animals."

The Need to Know

*1...Five "animal athletes," to use the term of the Professional Cowboys Rodeo Association, died at the California Rodeo in Salinas in July, 1995. This fact was completely ignored in the pro rodeo media.

Three of the deaths were in unsanctioned events: Two thoroughbred race horses reportedly died of broken legs and cardiac arrest though some of us suspect drug abuse may have been involved. Another horse ran into a fence post and broke his neck in the pandemonium of a "wild horse race," an event which should be banned.

In sanctioned events, a steer had his neck broken in the steer wrestling competition and was euthanized, and, most disturbing of all, a roping calf had his back broken by a jerk down. Although veterinarians were present, the calf was not humanely euthanized, but was sent off to slaughter, terrified and in agony.

No painkillers were given "for that would ruin the meat" said the attending vet. Does it seem reasonable for professional rodeo to adopt rules requiring immediate euthanasia for any animal in need thereof? The public expects it; common decency demands it, the future of pro rodeo depends on it. Any resulting financial loss should be considered part of the cost of doing business as a rodeo. (Note: the California rodeo brings Salinas a reported $16 million every year.)

*18 The year, 1998; the event, a news conference. The source of information, Mr. Cockerham, U.S. Department of Agriculture inspector at a plant in Nebraska, and Lester Friedlander, a veterinarian and meat plant employee. Cattle were skinned while still alive, screaming pigs were dunked in very hot water, and other animals were also tyrannized in the name of

The Need to Know

efficient production. The federal law is not ambiguous: Animals must be humanely killed before dismemberment, but productivity often has priority, and the law is ignored. Cockerham said he saw workers cut body parts of cattle that were still alive and conscious, and not just occasionally.

The plants do have inspectors: Inspectors dissuaded, according to Friedlander, by USDA officials from blowing the whistle, and from reporting inhumane treatment of animals. These conditions were the reason he left in 1995, he said.

*1 Six leading physicians from three different institutions, led by Dr. Louisa Chapman of the Centers for Disease Control and Prevention in Atlanta, argued in the *New England Journal of Medicine*-that medical professionals and policymakers "must recognize that although xenotrans-plantation the transfer of animal parts into humans promises benefits for specific patients, that promise is accompanied by an unquantifiable but undeniable potential for harm to the wider community," by enabling diseases such as AIDS, ebsola virus, and hanta virus to cross species barriers. Often a microorganism harmless in one species devastates another.

*1 Acting on a plea from the All India Animal Welfare Association of Bombay, the Karnataka High Court and Bangalore High Court in early January both banned a fox massacre held at the first full moon each year by the villages of Kadabal and Dhanaganhalli (near Bangalore) in honor of Sankranti, a local Hindu harvest deity. Traditionally dozens of foxes' mouths are sewn shut, and their left ears pierced with large golden earrings. After a chariot ride to the local temple followed by a drinking party, firecrackers are tied to the foxes' tails and detonated. Fleeing into the forest, the foxes' usually die of their

The Need to Know

wounds. The massacre is profane according to most interpretations of Hinduism, which in the strictest form forbids ever killing animals.

*1 Referring to the conduct of a technician at Huntington Life Sciences in East Millstone, New Jersey, Jeff Harington of the Cincinnati Enquirer made the following report."PETA's video shows technicians dangling monkeys, yelling at them, throwing some of them into cages and threading tubes down their noses. At one point a monkey displays movement and a quickened heartbeat when a technician cuts into his chest. The technician remarks,"this guy could be out a little more," as he continues to slice. PETA's complaint alleged the technician was conducting a necropsy on a live monkey.

* 4 "The breeding sow should be thought of and treated as a valuable piece of machinery whose function is to pump out baby pigs like a sausage machine." Words addressed to hog farmers, 1978. "Forget the pig is an animal. Treat him like a machine in a factory. Schedule treatments like you would lubrication. Breeding like the first step in an assembly line. And marketing like the delivery of finished goods." Words addressed to hog farmers, 1976

*1 Scalding a puppy to death is not a violent crime, a youth counselor ruled December 30,1993 in Brooksville, Texas, thereby preventing police from sending the 12-year-old suspect to a juvenile detention center. The youth showed no remorse and police believed "very strongly" that he was likely to commit another similar offense. The boy was charged with a third-degree felony.

The Need to Know

*1 In March, 1993 Mike Wallace defended biomedical researcher Michael Carey's cat-shooting experiments at the University of Louisiana on the January 25 episode of the CBS news program "60 Minutes," discrediting a witness who retracted a claim that she heard cats screaming in pain, but ignoring a General Accounting Office report that established the cats suffered pain and found that the whole $2.1 million project pointless. The cat shooting experiments were canceled in 1991. Other "60 Minutes" reporters, including fur opponent Andy Rooney, have done many stories friendly to animals.

*14 Can you empathize with an animal? Try; imagine that you are a calf somewhere in New Mexico. It's about 3 a.m. and 105 degrees in a world of dust, and the cows and their 253 babies bellow as they are being herded into a corral by the whoops and yells of cowboys. The cowboys then separate you and the other babies from their mothers, who are made to leave the corral.

What happens next is more difficult to imagine. You are roped by the hind legs and dragged and suddenly thrown to your right side: one man castrates you; another man inoculates into your leg; another into your backside and yet another cuts off a part of your ear. But it's not over. The branding iron burns your hair and skin, leaving your owner's visible symbol of ownership. This is a custom of torturous tyranny and the most terrible part is yet to come.

The Need to Know

*19   Reform is going to be an uphill battle, in India where more than 1000 bears are being "danced." Fewer than 8000 Sloth bears remain in the wild. The yearly capture of about 200 wild cubs for the dancing bear market contributes to the decline of this endangered species. Poachers sneak into dens while the mother bear is out and steal young cubs just weeks old. The initial shock of separation causes a 20% mortality rate. Surviving cubs are transported to markets in small wooden boxes without food or water. Many die en route. Those that reach the villages arrive traumatized and dehydrated. More than 40% of the cubs do not live to see their first birthday.

The cubs nose is pierced with a carpet needle. A rope is inserted through the delicate tissue and pulled down through the mouth. A second nose piercing is done at six months of age when the cubs snout is larger and cartilage in the upper palate is stronger and able to withstand a thicker rope. This time the rope is pulled out through the right or left nostril.

Infection following piercing is common. Re-piercing is necessary when the rope tears right through the flesh. At ten months when the adult canine teeth grow in, they are removed without anesthesia by hammering an iron rod into the tooth with a blunt end wooden pestle.

Bears are taught to walk on their hind legs by tugging on the rope that pierces their nose. Dancing is taught by twisting the rope and simultaneously pulling it up so that the squealing cub must pull itself up to reduce the pain on its muzzle. The bear's feet are struck by a stick and the bear learns to lift its feet to avoid further blows. Eventually the tapping of the stick on the ground is enough to make it move from one foot to the other. Bears work 12 hours a day without rest. They are fed an unnatural and deprived diet and spend much of their lives tethered with four-foot ropes. The bears are

The Need to Know

deprived of all that is natural to them. They are robbed of the freedom to make relationships with other bears, to roam the forest, to play and to sleep in peace. Most will be slaves for a lifetime. According to WSPA they are the only hope on the horizon for these tortured creatures.

*19 The animals in Haiti suffer tremendously as they try to continue their work. Many become lame and are either beaten to death or left to die. Perhaps the best way to illustrate the suffering of these working animals is through the words of a woman in Haiti who witnesses their daily burden. Kaitia Jean Pierre, a lifelong resident with a dedication for animal protection, tells of an incident which aptly describes the current crisis: "A donkey that fell not very far from me was so tired, skinny and was carrying a load so heavy it was almost as high as him. He fell and couldn't stand up. The woman that was guiding him started to beat him hardly. He had no reaction. I went to her, furious, and asked her to stop, saying that the animal was exhausted, that I had a car and would carry the loads wherever she wanted as long as she left the animal alone. She refused and continued to beat him, until, screaming with pain, he stood up, going from one side to the other like the inflated clowns they used for children to punch. They went away; I was so sad."

*1 Although it is not natural for a horse to run at high speeds for extended periods of time-even for three or four minutes-horses are forced to run at two years of age, long before their musculoskeletal systems have developed. The result of this pre-mature "exercise" is the fracturing of bones not strong enough to withstand grueling races. Drug abuse within the horse racing industries is rampant. And where do 75% of the young racehorses go when they can no longer race? To slaughter, of course. Racing is an $8.6 billion a year sport. The Omak Suicide Race in Washington State kills horses by running them at breakneck speeds down a cliff into water.

*13 The experiments were taped in 1985 at the State University of New York at Stony Brook. They show a series of live animals being fed to domesticated ferrets in crude predator behavior experiments. The undergraduate student who arranged these "kills" said that personal enjoyment was one of his motives. Mouse kill #1: A white mouse is thrown into the metal bathtub. He gets his bearings, using his whiskers to feel out the parameters of the tub corner where he has landed. The ferret sees him and approaches. Unable to get past the ferret towering over him the mouse goes between the ferret's legs, but is trapped. The kill begins. Mouse kill #2: A second mouse is thrown into the metal tub. The scene is repeated. Rat kill #3: A white, domesticated rat much larger than the mice who preceded him is thrown into the tub. He seems to sense the danger instantly and to look desperately about for an escape route he cannot hope to find. The ferret attacks but slips on the tub floor as the rat fights for his life, and the ferret seems unable to get a grip on his prey. The screams of the rat make the comments of the human observers hard to hear. The animals struggling for life and death cannot keep their footing on the slippery tub surface. Minutes later the rat stops screaming and lies still. Rabbit kill: A rabbit almost as large as the ferret is tossed into the tub. A mat of some sort has been placed on the floor now to allow the ferret to keep his footing during the attacks. His instincts aroused the ferret attacks the rabbit in a random fashion, digging his teeth into whatever part of the rabbit he can grasp. The rabbit is frantic, screaming loudly and pitifully kicking his legs, trying to escape, but the ferret hangs on. The struggle is long and horrible, the rabbit screaming throughout. After some minutes the ferret gets his tooth into the rabbit's eye and starts digging through his skull. The rabbit remains conscious. After nine minutes of suffering the rabbit is still alive and breathing.

*13 Sensitive primates, including many chimpanzees, are being subjected to painful disease experiments (including AIDS and hepatitis) at the SEMA laboratory in Rockville, Md. Many of the 600 animals confined at SEMA are kept in total isolation units where they often go insane. United States Department of Agriculture (USDA) reports still cite serious housing and veterinary care deficiencies that remain uncorrected. "'Touring SEMA was the worst experience of my life", Dr. Jane Goodall.

*13 A videotape obtained from an insider at East Carolina State University showed an inadequately anesthetized dog subjected to lengthy, painful and unnecessary surgery during a standard classroom exercise called "dog Lab." The tape showed the instructor joking as the dog cried out.

*13 Multinational Hazelton Laboratories and other facilities were found to be using a crude method of animal identification called "toe clipping," in which the toes of mice, guinea pigs, and other unanesthetized animals were cut off, resulting in severe pain and blood loss.

*21 Premarin, a widely prescribed estrogen substitute manufactured by Wyeth-Ayerst, contains pregnant mares' urine (PMU). An estimated 75,000 pregnant mares are confined during pregnancy in stalls so narrow they can barely move.

The Need to Know

Investigators touring PMU farms found horses with untreated wounds and respiratory problems, dehydrated mares fighting over a drink of water, and horses tethered so tightly they could not lie down at all. The foals born on PMU farms are considered byproducts; some replace their exhausted mothers and the rest are sold to slaughter. Hormone-replacement drugs made from plant sources or synthetics more closely mimic estrogen found in humans and at least three have FDA-approval for use in preventing osteoporosis.

*18 As reported by Neil Trent: Some of the worst cruelties I have ever found were in the Bahamas. I was sent to investigate dogs hung from trees and dogs who had their tongues cut out because "they barked too much." This sounds unspeakable but I have seen it with my own eyes. The suffering of these dogs haunts me.

*15 As reported in April, 1996: For the past 36 years a professor of neurophysiology at Rockefeller University, has claimed to be studying the pathways of nerve cell stimulation- particularly those involved with the inner ear and balance. In a typical experiment, the professor anesthetizes his helpless victims and inserts tubes, electrodes, and transducers throughout their bodies, allowing him to drug and manipulate the cats in any way he chooses.

Next he cuts the cerebrum of the cats (the portion of the brain that controls higher functioning) from the spinal cord, supposedly to stop sensations of pain and awareness -even though medical and scientific experts question whether this procedure really blocks all awareness of the animal. That done, the professor discontinues the anesthesia and paralyzes the cats with drugs. To study neck rotation, the professor suspends the cats by hip pins and a spinal clamp while ce-

The Need to Know

menting the animals' heads to a computer-driven head rotator. After carving open their spinal cords, he connects electrodes to exposed muscles and nerves to administer electric shocks. Following hours and sometimes days of this "science" the professor's "preparations" are finally killed.

It is at the same school that another professor of neurophysiology has induced vomiting in conscious and unconscious cats killing over 250 cats. This vivisector proceeds by severing the brain and paralyzing the cats. Then he pumps nausea-inducing drugs into the animals in doses hundreds of times greater than those any human would receive. Because of the paralysis, the cats can't vomit. The response of the nerves that would normally result in vomiting are observed. In another experiment a cat, was forced to vomit 97 times in a 3 ½ hour period! And then the cat was killed.

*13 Shoving a tube down a duck's throat, the factory farmer pumps the duck full of feed three times a day until the duck's liver swells to six times its normal size (or until the duck's internal organs burst.) Then the duck's throat is slit and his diseased, fatty liver is served as the "delicacy" foie gras.

*16 In Arizona, hunters pay good money to join in a hunt with the sole purpose of killing as many mountain lions, bobcats, coyotes, and foxes as they can in 100 days. The person who kills the most animals wins $10,000 in cash!

Hunt promoters are offering big-money prizes like this, based on a cruel scoring system that's guaranteed to put some of these animals on the endangered species list in a few years. The numbers of mountain lions and bobcats are already dwindling. To make sure these wild animals are ultimately wiped out (and inadvertently show to the rest of us what they're really up to) the promoters give hunters more points for killing females. Without their mothers, cubs starve to death or become even easier targets for killing. The threat is enormous. It is estimated that each "winner" will kill over 100 animals. And there are hundreds of hunters trying to win. If these hunts are allowed to continue, the slaughter could be in the tens of thousands.

*12 Every year the Museum of Science and Industry in Chicago receives approximately 8,000 fertile chicken eggs. These eggs are placed in a hatchery and then put on public display just before the chicks begin to hatch. The public then is able to watch the chicks peck through their shells for the next three weeks. Expecting the warmth of a mother hen, the chicks are surprised to find nothing but a metal grate. The young chickens are then sent to Lincoln Park Zoo to be used as "nutrition for the reptiles in the collection." The museum does not note this fact in the exhibit or in its fundraising materials. Most children think the chicks are sent to a farm.

*12 The American Veterinary Association (AVMA) currently endorses the inhumane farming practice of forced molting. Forced molting is the practice of intentionally starving millions of hens up to two weeks, until they lose 25% to 35% of their body weight in an effort to manipulate the hen's hormones to increase their egg production. Forced molting also increases the risk of bone breakage and is the cause of death for hundreds of thousands of hens each year.

In addition, forced molting impairs the immune system, predisposing hens and their eggs to Salmonella. According to a report by USDA immunologist Peter Holt, a healthy unmolten hen would have to ingest 50,000 salmonella cells in order to become infected compared to a molten hen that would become infected, by fewer than 10 cells. The AVMA is allegedly endorsing the starvation of hens solely to produce more eggs so farmers can make more money.

*17 Veterinarian Preech Puangkam, Director of the hospital at the Elephant Conservation Center in Lampang, Thailand is working against great odds. He is working day and night to help elephants who have been worked nearly to death, drugged, abandoned, or in other ways horribly abused by human beings. Elephants arrive at the hospital with festering wounds from having their tusks sawed off for ivory. Other elephants are nearly dead from exhaustion, having been pumped full of amphetamines and worked almost to death by illegal loggers.

Some elephants are simply abandoned when they cannot work anymore. Then they are often shot for encroaching on farms for food. The future of elephants in Thailand is grim.

At the turn of the century there were about 100,000 domesticated elephants in Thailand. Hundreds of thousands still roamed wild. Experts now estimate that there are now only about 2,000 elephants in the wild and about 5,000 in the domestic population. Preech fears that all wild elephants will be extinct in Thailand within 15 years.

*19 Bull Fights Performed in Spain in the Last Ten Years:

1985	492
1986	440
1987	456
1988	509
1989	513
1990	541
1991	583
1992	587

1993	630
1994	720

*16 Number of Animals Killed Annually in U.S.
- Fur 4-5 million
- Shelters 5.4 Million +
- Dissection 18 million
- Research & Testing 20 Million
- Hunting 200 Million
- Farmed Animals 9 Billion

*1 San Francisco Cruelty legal, "says judge;" "Just ducky," say politicians. No part of this title shall be construed ...to interfere with the right to kill all animals used for food. By making this the law of California in 1905, and refusing to amend it since then, the people have spoken: humans have the right to kill all food animals. If they can reasonably kill the animal with little or no physical pain, they should choose that method. However, if the slaughter involves physical pain to the animal that is not reasonably avoidable, food animals can still be killed under these conditions as well.

*11 Bare facts about the bear trade: Bear gallbladders are worth up to $6,000 each. Bear paws, a culinary delicacy among Chinese communities throughout the world, can sell for $180.00 per kg.(equivalent to 2.2046 pounds.) Illegal bear products find large markets in China, Japan, Korea, Singapore, Taiwan, and Thailand. Hunters kill about 41,000 black bears in the United States and Canada under legal quotas, but it is estimated that the illegal slaughter for export of bear parts involves at least another 41,000 bears. Bear farms are found in China and Korea, where bears are kept just for extraction of their bile. Taiwanese farmers want to reinstate the practice. The markets being served are not only in the Far East, but in immigrant communities within the United States and Canada.

*11 An International Wildlife Coalition survey of Toronto, Canada found bear gallbladders for sale in many stores and anecdotal evidence abounds that "sport" hunts in the United States are often cover-ups for the real purpose in killing bears: gallbladders. In fact, North Carolina researchers were appalled to find that poachers had stolen radio tracking devices so that black bears could be easily located and slaughtered for their paws and gall bladders.

*11 Brazil loses 12 million wild animals per year to the illegal wildlife trade; 90% of them die while being transported and do not even reach the market for which they are intended. IWC Brazil continues to do its best to counter these abuses.

*4 To Luke A. Dommer they were Bowbarians. "Bowhunters" he wrote, "claim to hunt with bows and arrows in order to give animals a sporting chance. True hunters completely miss their pray nine out of ten times even at close range, but eventually they make random hits. That means an arrow can accidently strike anywhere: The animal's neck, lungs, spine or leg, and rarely a vital spot; the heart for example, where the kill would be instant. Even then, archers still claim that deer usually die within thirty seconds from such hits.

Class A archer, (we call him Buck Doe) describes his bow hunt. "The arrow went through the doe's neck. We all saw it strike, and we all saw it sticking out of both sides as she bounded away. We came to several pools of blood with prints of her knees besides them where she had gone down to hang her head and bleed in the bright sun. We saw spots where she had stumbled. But still her life's blood ran, and still she went on. At last we found her, and she was dying. She was on her knees and hocks. Her ears, no longer the wonderful alert warning system, were sagging. Her head was down, her nose was in her blood. Some how the doe lurched up. Stumbling, bounding, crashing blindly through the brush, she managed to reach the rim of the plateau we were on and disappear. We fanned out and combed the hillside. We failed. I vowed never to hunt with a bow again."

And what about the deer who are struck by arrows and recovered, do they fare any better? Not really, because there is rarely, if ever, an instant kill in bow- hunting. Animals die from hemorrhaging; they bleed to death.

#11 An unhealthy, emaciated black bear was live- trapped in an Ontario, Canada backyard. Close medical attention followed, revealing something that felt very hard within the muscle of his neck. Knowing the object was foreign, the veterinarian proceeded to operate. To her astonishment, a portion of the shaft of an arrow was removed. As she cut deeper, she found the main reason for this bear's poor condition and the reason he was seeking an easy food source from human establishments. More cutting...and blood mixed with purulence from a severe infection revealed a steel arrowhead. The arrow had been a source of excruciating pain and discomfort for at least two months. The arrow, a result of a careless hunter during the controversial Spring Bear Hunt in Ontario, was slowly killing this once strong and proud male bear. Recovery took several months.

#11 In the early Ontario spring, outfitters who run canned hunts lure hungry bears to feeding stations known as bait sites with garbage meat. Some outfitters and guides continue to bait throughout the summer and fall.

As the warmer weather makes natural foods more available, the outfitters switch to sweets, such as stale cakes and pastries, which bears find irresistible. Killing bears over bait is the most profitable kind of bear hunting and occurs from April 15 to June 30, and from September 1 to November 30. The hunters, many dressed in combat gear, hide safely in blinds that are usually 10 to 20 meters away from the bait, waiting for a bear to appear. The area between the blind and the bait is cleared of vegetation to provide a clean shot. Hunters are supposed to wait and assess the size and the sex of the bear. However, according to a 1991 hunting article in *Field and Stream*, "harvest statistics indicate that most bait hunters actually settle for the first bear that shows up."

The hunter has his trophy photograph taken with the dead bear before and after the bear has been gutted and strung up. He now has proof that he has joined the bear hunting fraternity.

Females are often taken as trophies. When cubs leave the den, they are three to four months old and weigh 3 to 4kg (6 to 9 pounds) so they have little chance of survival without their mother. Once orphaned, they are killed by predators or they slowly starve to death. Their deaths are not recorded.

* 11 "...as an infant, the little male orangutan watched as his mother was killed and then cut up and dried in order to make orangutan jerky."

The famous orangutan researcher, Dr. Birute Galdikal, described the ordeal of a little orphaned orangutan, suffering severe depression in these words.

In what the United Nations has described as the worst environmental disaster of the last decade of the century, over 6,000 square miles of forest were obliterated during last year's forest fires. Poachers have been taking advantage of the chaos and of the orangutan's panic. They have been using rifles and machetes to kill orangutan mothers who were driven from the burning forests and who had approached human settlements. The babies are wrenched from the dying mother's arms to be sold in the black market pet trade.

*13 Investigation showed Puerto Rico, "The Shining Star of the Caribbean," to be a black hole for animals. Tourists and caring residents are haunted by the suffering they have witnessed and see every day. Starving dogs, cats, and even horses, roam the streets of every town on the island. If they don't die of hunger, thirst, or being hit by cars (their bodies litter the streets and highways,) dogs often succumb to distemper, parvo virus, or mange.

PETA investigator Teresa Gibbs reports: "When I got to Puerto Rico this is what I saw: Many of the dogs looked like walking skeletons their weak bodies thin, as they hobble about in search of food or a kind person. Those with mange are covered with bloody scabs from the tips of their noses to the tips of their tails. One particularly debilitated dog had lost almost all of the skin on her feet from the mange. When I picked her up, blood streamed down the front of my shirt. I looked down and saw that her feet were practically disintegrating from the disease. Many have been kicked and stoned by so many people that they run when approached, or scream when approached, or scream when touched by even the gentlest hand. Shop owners and farmers put out poison to kill the dogs, but the stream of abandoned animals seems endless. Because animal shelters are few and far between, and because some of the shelters are nothing more than warehouses where animals are left to die of disease or injury unattended in their cages, people have an expression for what to do with unwanted animals: they throw them away.... At the municipal pound in Ponce, I witnessed several animals dying on the cage floors while city workers wrung their hands, not knowing how to help. The veterinarian was not visiting that day. Records showed more than 60 animals had died in their cages from disease and injury in one month. Survivors are often given to the local medical school for experiments. Others are simply unaccounted for." (Teresa Gibbs met with representatives from the mayor's office and requested immediate action.)

*1 On May 15, 1998, United Animal Nations offered $1000 for information leading to the arrest of whoever dumped the remains of 43 greyhounds, three rabbits, and a cat near O'Fallon, Missouri, in mid-April. Most of the greyhounds were puppies whose ears had been cut off to remove identifying tattoos.

*7 1905 saw the publication of Upton Sinclair's The Jungle, a book depicting the horrors of the slaughterhouse. For the first time, Americans read about appalling work conditions and diseased meat products and-they learned that live, fully conscious animals were being hoisted by one leg, kicking and screaming as their throats were slit, and bled to death. The public was appalled and demanded reform, and they got it. In 1906, Congress passed the "Federal Meat Inspection Act," which required meat to be inspected for human health hazards. It took another 50 years before humane concerns were addressed, and the "Humane Slaughter Act" was finally passed in 1958. The law requires that animals be stunned before slaughter. But the law does not require the meat, dairy, egg, and poultry industries to be compassionate, or even concerned about animal suffering, and they are neither. Blatant slaugh-

The Need to Know

terhouse cruelties are documented in the industries's own publications and-U.S. Department of Agriculture reports, yet no slaughterhouse has ever been prosecuted for failing to abide by humane slaughter regulations.

In 1989, Dr. Temple Grandin, a livestock industry consultant and researcher, visited 20 slaughterhouses across the United States. Among the welfare problems she witnessed, one plant hung "live crippled hogs that hadn't been stunned on a shackle line; two large beef plants had slick floors and broken chutes: Cattle skidded and fell down on the slick floors; at two other slaughterhouses, the captive bolt stunners had lost enough power that they were unable to deliver full impact by the end of the shift."

Dr. Grandin has extensively researched stunning problems at slaughterhouses and her findings are alarming. Currently the industry uses three methods to stun animals: captive bolt stunning (whereby a gun that shoots a bolt into the animals brain;) cardiac arrest electrical stunning; and head-only electrical stunning. All three methods can cause tremendous pain and suffering. If captive bolt guns are improperly placed or if the gun is poorly maintained, the animals are not stunned, and will be in severe pain from a partial impact. Cardiac arrest stunning kills the animals by stopping the heart, and animals can feel painful heart attack symptoms. Insufficient cardiac electrical stunning also results in paralyzed animals that feel everything. Many small plants use head-only stunning because they lack restraint equipment.

This type of stunning is reversible, and animals regain consciousness when they are not bled immediately due to slow hoist or other handling problems. The most severe stunning problems occurred in calf slaughterhouses. According to Dr. Grandin, "Approximately half of the calf slaughterers in the U.S. shackle calves while they are still alive, despite the fact that this is illegal. When stunning methods were used, they were often inadequate. Calf slaughterhouses frequently use head-only electrical stunning, and the animals often regain consciousness before and during bleeding. Cardiac arrest stunning of young calves (called Bob calves) is anything but humane. Twenty to forty percent of Bob calves stunned by cardiac arrest have eye reflexes, and some continue to vocalize. Captive bolt stunning is more accurate, but some packers do not want to use captive bolt stunning because it destroys the calf brains which are a marketable product. Horrible animal suffering continues because profits, not animal welfare, guides slaughterhouse practice. Poor stunning procedures and lack of enforcement should be enough to convince anyone that the "Humane Slaughter Act" is anything but humane. The law is problematic for even more reasons.

The "Humane Slaughter Act" specifically exempts poultry, (which comprise ninety percent of all animals killed for food production), and ritual slaughter, such as kosher (Jewish) and halal (Muslim). Kosher and halal slaughter require that the animals be fully conscious at the time of death. At ritual slaughterhouses, a chain is wrapped around one of the animal's rear legs and the frightened, conscious animal is hoisted into the air, kicking and thrashing. Large animals, such as cattle, are particularly prone to torn ligaments and broken bones during this "humane" process. Dr. Grandin, who has been allowed to visit ritual slaughter plants, wrote: "...after visiting one plant in which five steers were hung up in a row to await slaughter, I had nightmares. The animals were hitting the walls and their bellowing could be heard in the parking lot. In some plants the suspended animal's head is restrained by a nosetong connected to an air cylinder. Stretching the neck by pulling on the nose is painful. Suspension upside down also causes great discomfort"

Live shackle and hoist slaughter methods are considered so archaic and cruel that they have been banned in other countries. To date, despite documented slaughterhouse cruelties, the U.S. Government has done little to prevent blatant animal abuse at packing plants. With faster slaughter lines and new technology such as chemical "dehairing," it is likely to get worse.

Over 30 years have passed since the first attempt to make slaughter "more humane," evidence that the legislation has not worked speaks for itself.

*11 It took no time at all for (South African) Government gunmen to kill the parents of the baby elephant as it snoozed in the riverside shade.

At first the adult elephants were merely curious about the hovering helicopter. Even the first gunshots failed to unsettle them. It was only when the mother sank to her knees with a pitiful wail that the awful truth began to dawn. But there was no time to run. Within seconds, blood was also streaming from the father. Meanwhile, the officially hired guns of the Kruger National Park Board were moving in to whisk away the elephant calf for sale, the fate of many other young victims of this national barbarism.

On that particular day in June, 1995, 300 African elephants were slaughtered. Adults were strung up and sold as carcasses to be rendered into dog food, their feet turned into umbrella stands, tails made into fly whisks, and their tusks put into a growing ivory stockpile. During the butchering process, a fetus lay on the ground as a disemboweled female was winched by her trunk into a flatbed truck. Witnesses to this carnage say it haunts them forever.

Dozens of newly orphaned calves, dazed with fear and

shock, were rounded up and sold that same day to foreign zoos or circuses for a life in captivity. The babies are scarred for life by the trauma they experienced.

*4 Up until 600 years ago, at the end of the Koryo dynasty most Koreans followed Buddhist tradition and people were encouraged to abstain from all meats. But now, two million dogs (thirty percent of them former family companions) are brutally caged, killed, and consumed by human beings every year. In South Korea, an overpopulation of dogs is nonexistent. All strays and homeless dogs are captured by butchers and sold on the open market.

Severely impoverished people began eating dogs about 50 years ago, but only in the past 20 years has dog eating become an exploding practice. Only in 1988, when Korean dog eating came under attack by worldwide animal protection activists, and amid growing threats of an Olympic Games boycott did the Korean media defend the practice as a centuries long tradition. Dog meat dealers vigorously promoted dog flesh for good health, stamina, and as a sexual enhancing food that would last its consumer several years.

Although the majority of South Koreans condone the eating of dogs, only 2 to 3% of the total population consumes them on a regular basis. During bok days, "Korean summer hot dog days," beginning in the middle of July and ending in early August, about 1,000 dogs are sold to consumers on a daily basis, at just one market. After being chosen by a consumer, (as are lobsters in the United States), a dog is captured in the cage by a noose and then dragged into the street or into the open and beaten over the head by the butcher with an iron pipe or hammer. To make certain the dog is dead, an electric stick is used to shock the animal to death. Prior to electric stunning, the dogs, having already seen other dogs

124

The Need to Know

slaughtered before them, struggle in vain after capture, yelping and pitifully howling as they fight valiantly for their lives. But after several blows to the head-sometimes up to five-the dogs are finally rendered unconscious and the electrocution can begin. Each blow by the iron pipe or hammer causes the dog to scream, while the consumer nonchalantly watches on. The carcass is then thrown into a vat of boiling water, a high whirlpool machine designed to remove its fur, and is then browned by a blow torch.

Dogs are similarly marketed in the Philippines. The methods employed to restrain the animals and prevent their barking are hauntingly cruel. Their sale has been banned in Metro Manila, the capital, and in Baguo, the northern capital, after protests by animal protectionists.

*4 The following excerpts are from a report by Jonathan Pierce, coordinator for The World Society for the Protection of Animals WSPA.

In India, concern over the spread of rabies results in the brutal destruction of hundreds of thousands of dogs every year. One minute a dog is asleep under a palm tree; the next it is dragged by its neck into the back of a van and clubbed unconscious....Unfortunately for many dogs, just as for other animals and large sections of the human population, the streets are their home. To the casual observer it would be easy to assume that these animals are all strays-unwanted scavengers, struggling to survive on whatever they find. But this would be a mistake; most dogs seen in the streets of India have very clearly defined territories and are regarded as companions by many members of the community....This summer I witnessed the methods employed to control the dog population in India's fourth largest city, Madras.

The Madras Corporation employs about 20 people at a

The Need to Know

dog pound north of the city center. From here, four vans fan out to different parts of the city each morning. I followed one van for several hours as it wove its way through the crowded streets of the city, searching for dogs. Soon the van stopped near a busy market and one of the catchers got out and approached a light brown mongrel. The owner of a nearby cafe and some of his customers immediately shouted at the catcher to leave the dog alone. It was a neighborhood dog and residents clearly didn't want it killed. (The dog catchers received the same reaction on several occasions, and in one incident the van was the target of stone throwers.)

But for many other dogs there was no one nearby to defend them. In less than thirty seconds they were lassoed with a string, dragged by the neck along the street and thrown into the van. Those who put up the most resistance always came off worst. One large mongrel was so determined to escape that it took all the catcher's strength to haul it into the van. I looked in through a caged window and saw the catcher beating the dog over the head with a club. Five, six, seven times he struck the animal; the thump of the club and the cries of the dog echoed through the narrow street; finally, after the tenth blow, the animal fell unconscious. At the back of the van I saw the dogs caught earlier in the day cowering in fear. In Madras, about 100 dogs are caught this way every day.

At the pound dogs are kept until the next day and then destroyed so owners have only a few hours to reclaim them once they are missing. The morning I visited the pound, the extermination was being carried out to an unrelenting schedule.

Dogs were being dragged one after another from filthy kennels as if they were on a production line. Most were killed by electrocution in a chamber more than 50 years old (many

The Need to Know

of the chambers were exported from England during the 1930s after they had been outlawed there.) Inside the electrocution room the smell of burnt fur was overpowering. The screams of each dog intensified as its neck was bound tightly with a steel chain, which was then hooked up to the main electrical supply in the chamber. After the dog was doused with a bucket of water (to enhance the electrical current), the chamber door was closed and an electrician threw the switch to deliver five separate shocks to kill the dog. After a minute it was removed and thrown on an accumulating pile of carcasses....If sufficient current is delivered through the brain of the animal, death can be painless and instantaneous. But the device used in Madras sends the electricity through the body, not through the brain, and the power supply is extremely variable. Under these circumstances death can be prolonged and agonizing; in some instances death does not come at all.

Local animal welfare workers testified that on occasion they had pulled dogs from a pile of carcasses and found them still alive....In some cities, lethal injection of magnesium sulfate is used, which is extremely cheap, and is usually administered to dogs in the street. Before the animal dies, it suffers several minutes of violent convulsions, during which time it can be heard and seen whining, howling, and gasping for air. Strychnine is also widely used in India, distributed in the streets disguised as rice or chappaties.

The dogs who take this bait endure at least fifteen minutes of excruciating muscle contractions before dying of heart failure....Director Christine Townsend, who runs the animal's shelter in Jaipur, described the effects of the drug. "You know when strychnine has been used because suddenly all the dogs in the neighborhood disappear. In one instance we came across deep hollows in the ground which the dogs had clawed out in an attempt to relieve their agony." In one suburb of Madras, the Cleansing Department rounds up dogs and throws them into the back of rubbish carts. About fifty dogs are crammed in each cart and then a small amount of cyanide is scattered on top. It takes about half an hour for all the dogs to perish. Across India these brutal methods are used day after day on hundreds of dogs. About 30,000 are killed each year in the Madras execution chamber alone; at least another 10,000 are killed in outlying parts of the city. In Bombay 55,000 dogs were killed in 1992; in Delhi 78,000, and in Jaipur 3,600 were destroyed.

*5 The Department of Defense causes more pain to the animals in its laboratories than any other laboratory user in the United States. According to a 1986 Office of Technology Assessment report, 84 percent of the animals used in military experiments were used in painful or noxious experiments.... The situation in military laboratories is as grim as animal experiments can get. Animals are hit with chemical weapons, radiation, and, of course, bullets, both low and high velocity. Animals are also used in countless other kinds of experiments. And problems are rampant.

　　Former research facility staff members and veterinarians cite poor animal care and neglect at military facilities. Many doctors and former researchers have leveled charges of cruelty, redundancy, irrelevance, and improper extrapolation of data from animals to humans. The military peer review process is weak; some military experiments may duplicate research conducted in the civilian centers....

　　The Letterman Army Institute of Research is one of the sites of abysmal conditions for animals. Christina Vancheri, a civilian illustrator at LAIR from 1979 to 1984, found that monkeys used in visual experiments were kept *permanently* in restraint chairs. Monkeys used in doctor's experiments were

128

restrained up to *three* years, and animal "health records" revealed that others have been restrained for as long as *twelve* years. The International Primate Protection League reviewed autopsy reports for LAIR and revealed several instances of neglect.

An 11-month-old Rhesus female was found dying in her cage, having lost 10 to 12 percent of her weight due to dehydration caused by a malfunctioning water system that was not noted by veterinarians or animal caretakers. An 8-month-old male Rhesus monkey died of causes which included "anemia due to louse infestation."

*16 The Associated Press, Salisbury, Pa. "The cries of caged dogs drown out the sounds of chickens and cows on Ivan Stolzfus" farm. About 50 animals with matted coats sit crammed together two and three to each small cage, clawing frantically at the wire walls as they try to perch on mesh floors. They shake uncontrollably; they cower to the human touch. The dogs are not pets. They are a lucrative industry for Stolzfus and fellow farmers. The animals breeding on farms like Stolzfus' spend their short lives in cages, giving birth twice a year to litters of purebreds that are fast becoming Pennsylvania's most profitable cash crop.... The vast majority of the dogs sold in pet shops-up to half a million a year-are bred in puppy mills that are notorious for their cramped, crude, and filthy conditions. Puppy mill kennels consist of small wood and wire mesh cages, usually kept outdoors with no shelter from the blistering sun or bitter cold winds. Female dogs are bred continuously, and are often starving and dehydrated because of the enormous drain on their systems by the never ending cycle of puppies they nurse. Sadly, these mothers are killed at the age of six or seven, when their bodies give out and they no longer can produce enough litters.

The Need to Know

Puppies are separated from their mothers at the age of 4 to 8 weeks and sold to brokers who pack them in crates for transport and resale to pet stores. Between unsanitary conditions at puppy mills and poor treatment in transport, only half the puppies make it to pet stores alive.

The USDA claims that it simply doesn't have the resources to inspect puppy mills, much less prosecute the facilities that violate the Animal Welfare Act.

*5 The Department of Defense agency funds about $20 million worth of experiments every year, mainly at the Armed Forces Radiobiology Research Institute (AFRRI) in Bethesda, Maryland, where gruesome experiments have continued year after year. In 1985, thirty nine monkeys were irradiated to see if higher radiation doses affected how long they survived or the degree of their incapacitation.

Another experiment was so abusive that it was hard to believe it took place as recently as 1987. Sixty-six mice were divided into three groups. One group was subject to radiation. A second group had 30% of their skin cut off with a steel punch. A third group was soaked with alcohol, then lit on fire and allowed to burn for 12 seconds. Other mice received combinations of these abusive treatments. The experimental results? Irradiated mice are less active and eat poorly. Burned mice drink more water. Those who are irradiated and burned recover more quickly than those who are irradiated and have much of their skin cut away....more than 60,000 animals were used in that year alone. Although the stated goals of the experiments are to try to develop ways to protect soldiers from radiation effects or to improve treatments, the program mainly demonstrates in animals what was already known from human exposure.

The Need to Know

*15 Bion was a joint U.S./Russian/French project that launched two monkeys into space during July, 1996 for a sixteen-day flight to measure changes in their physiology. The monkey's "training" includes being straightjacked while 14 different cables are burrowed under their skin, after which they are forced to sit for over two weeks without relief in a restraining device. NASA's chief veterinarian, Sharon Vanderlip, resigned, citing non-compliance with federal animal welfare laws, and her frustration with NASA's refusal to allow her to make changes.

*15 Each year at certain Native American reservations live roosters are mutilated and killed during a rooster pull. During the event, a live rooster is partially buried in dirt or secured to a tree as men on horseback tear at the rooster and beat each other with it.

*11 Pat Gray's determined investigation into the Spring 1988 Canadian seal hunt turned up hundreds--perhaps thousands--of cases of unparalleled and vindictive butchery. March 10,1988: Even though the Department of Fisheries and Oceans continues to assure us there will be no hunt off Prince Edward Island, rumors persist. A total of 275,000 Harp seals and 10,000 hooded seals may be killed this season under the official quota.
March 23, 1998: There have been reports of extreme cruelty and barbaric behavior by certain individuals who were alleged to have cut off the flippers of several pups, rolling them over and over with their feet, kicking them, and eventually leaving them to bleed to death in agony. The flippers were later hung like trophies from several-pick up trucks. Numerous reports of animals "skinned" alive penis bones tied to car radio antennas, and an adult seal half skinned and

bloody, still alive, being dragged behind a truck. The four occupants of the truck were covered in blood and yelling out the window.

March 26,1998: There are many sealing vessels patrolling the waters north of the island, slaughtering seals from the main herd, working fast before the wind changes. The herd cannot possibly sustain the high numbers of this year's quota.

Pristine ice floes, just over the horizon, a few miles off the north shore of beautiful Prince Edward Island, are flowing with blood, all for the sake of the "Canadian Rite of Spring" in defiance of world opinion.

March 27,1998: A few sealers appear to be carrying rifles, but the majority seem to be using clubs.

*11 March 30,1998 Times and Transcript: By Ron Ward and Dave Francis....the battle is between the seals and the hunters. It is a one-sided battle. We watch as a crew from a 17-meter sealing ship efficiently kills as many as 60 or 70 seals resting on an ice field...It takes little time: the men move across the ice, sometimes swinging back-hand as they walk through groups of three or four. Striking the seals in the head is the method of choice, and has proven to be in most cases quick and effective. But many times we watch as sealers strike seals twice, three times, four times before killing them. It is a bizarre ballet on ice that is repeated endlessly throughout the day. It is not a scene for the squeamish or weak of heart. The sealers prefer not to be watched or photographed, fearing the story will be sensationalized by the media. Death, blood, cruelty, and: the public they know, will be spellbound by the images.

April 2,1998- Some seal kill stats: Most recent reports from the Department of Fisheries and Oceans-93,809.(Last

The Need to Know

year at this time the kill was 39,924.) We'll only know what this means at the end of the season, but it doesn't look good for the seals.

In Souris harbor, 7 Newfoundland sealing vessels were docked. One of the vessels had pelts stacked so high on deck, it looked as though it might turn over in a rough sea.

April 7,1998, Report #2-Seals are coming ashore by the thousands along the north shore. We have seen around 200 animals today, white coats, raggedy jackets, beaters, bluebacks...most have only a hole where the penis was removed, the skulls are uncrushed and exposed, and some have a clean spiral cut around the whole body. The carnage and waste of young lives is atrocious...these people are barbarians!

*1 "A 22 year-old horse was repeatedly raped, tortured, and in the end, butchered at the Western College of Veterinary Medicine, Saskatoon Saskatchewan, Canada over a period of several weeks," an anonymous letter to **Animal People** alleged. It came with shocking documentation from the March 1997 edition of the Canadian Veterinary Journal. Wrote researchers Clair E. Card, Stephen T. Manning, Pam Bowman, and Taryn Leibel: "Both forelimbs of the emaciated horse trembled when bearing weight. Bilateral carpal enlargement was present, and both joints were displaced...The stallion had extreme difficulty in balancing when a foreleg was lifted. The left forelimb had a valgus deformity. The flexor tendors of both forelegs were chronically bowed. The horse walked reluctantly, using a slow shuffling gait. The master problem list included poor body condition, chronic obstructive pulmonary disease, cardiac disease, chronic musculoskeletal disease of the forelimbs, and generalized weakness." Despite all that, and evident poor libido, the researchers reported "breeding or semen collection was attempted for about six weeks using natural cover, manual stimulation, artificial vagina, pharmacologic induction of ejaculation, and electro-ejaculation. After the latter, involving the insertion of an electrode into the horses rectum, the horse stretched out into lateral recumbency, and suffered cardiac arrest." Translation: he died.

*11 "Fast food" in some parts of Asia can mean a bear paw hacked off that morning from a living animal kept in a cage at the back of the restaurant. Bears paws fetch about $70 each in Asian markets.

Many come from wild black or grizzly bears in North America. Cubs of Asiatic black (moon) bears and the beautiful Asian sun bears are swept up by poachers in Burma, Laos, and Cambodia. Their fate may be to suffer for years in a small cage in China, a tube in their stomach draining their bile...or to have their paws hacked off, one at a time, for hungry businessmen in Korea...or to be kept near starvation in circuses or zoos.

*16 The story was in the newspapers of El Sobrante, California. Two boys had ruthlessly tortured a stray dog called Sunshine, a golden-haired dog the whole neighborhood had taken to their hearts when she first appeared out of nowhere. According to the grim account the two boys had taken Sunshine-a dog they had played with only days before-to a secluded wooded area behind the condominium complex where they lived. The teenagers tied one end of a rope around Sunshine's neck and the other to an over hanging branch, so she couldn't move without choking. Then they made a makeshift blow torch out of an aerosol can and a lighter. Repeatedly they burned the helpless dog as she howled in pain. Each time Sunshine struggled to get free, the rope around her neck got

The Need to Know

tighter and tighter. When the boys finally tired of their "fun" with the blowtorch, they took turns shooting Sunshine with a pellet gun they had brought along for the occasion.By the time they were finished, they had fired nearly 60 pellets into the dog's head, blinding her. The boys showed no remorse.

*1 Shocked at the treatment of six giant sea turtles they found cruelly tied awaiting slaughter at a feast held for New Zealand prime minister Jim Bolger in the Marshall Islands, TV reporters kept their cameras rolling as, to their further horror, the turtles were roasted on hot coral and butchered alive. Bolger avoided eating the turtle meat. Asked for comment by New Zealand Herald reporter Catherine Masters, Australian sea turtle biologist Colin Limpus took the opportunity to denounce not only the turtle killing, but also the common practice of boiling alive lobsters and crayfish.

*1 Increased pressure on illegal badger baiters and dog fighters is driving them out of England and Wales, into less populated Scotland, according to British police. "From 9000 to 10,000 badgers a year are killed in staged fights with dogs," says Jery Brookes, chair of the National Federation of Badger Groups. "A fully grown badger is more than a match for any single dog," explains wildlife liaison officer Sgt. Graham Young, "but they are usually faced with two dogs, and fresh dogs are put in all the time. The outcome is always death for the badger." Poachers sell badgers to baiting rings for as much as $2,000 apiece.

*1 "If we start going with morals and ethics, we might as well put everything away and let the anti hunting crowd take over." Dan Heal of the California Sportsmen Task Force told reporters, after the state Fish and Game Director Commission

rejected Fish and Game director Boyd Gibbons recommen-
dation that it ban bear hunting with dogs.

*1 A Cincinnati activist group got its start when a member,
John Rockwell, discovered through the Freedom of Information Act that a veterinarian was experimenting on beagles
for Proctor & Gamble in a lab behind his animal hospital. For
several months the small group picketed the veterinarian.

*7 The mangled body of a cow was found in a high school
parking lot in Boonville, N. Y. The police investigated the
matter and determined that the cow had been stolen from a
dairy farm, chained to the back of a truck, and dragged several miles to her death. Upon learning of the atrocity, Farm
Sanctuary urged the authorities to take action and offered a
reward for information leading to the arrest and conviction
of the responsible parties. It took over a year, but it now
appears that those responsible will be brought to justice.

*12 In 1997, The Irish SPCA (Society for The Prevention of
Cruelty to Animals) And the Royal SPCA conducted an undercover investigation of the Spanish Greyhound racing industry. The groups inspected race tracks, kennels, and animals that are housed at those facilities. At the conclusion of
the investigation, Mike Butcher, Chief Inspector of the Royal
SPCA's special operation unit, said. "We found appalling suffering because basic welfare steps are ignored."

Finbarr Heslin, the chief veterinarian on the project,
documented dozens of instances where inadequate steps were
taken to assure the welfare of the animals. In his report, he
stated that greyhounds:
 •   are infested with parasites,
 •   are not given adequate veterinary care,

The Need to Know

- are forced to sleep on bare concrete with no bedding,
- are kept in cages 15 to 18 inches wide,
- are routinely given amphetamines, caffeine, corticosteroid, anabolic steroids, and cocaine.

In addition, the report noted that some dogs are forced to share a kennel so small that only one dog could lay down, forcing the other to stand all the time. It was also noted that many dogs are forced to race while injured, wearing bandages for support or to cover wounds.

Another undercover investigation found that once that dogs are no longer productive in the greyhound industry they are sold to hunters. The dogs are used throughout the hunting season to assist hunters in stalking prey. At the conclusion of the season the greyhounds are killed. It is more economical for hunters to get a new greyhound at the beginning of the next season, than to feed the animal throughout the year.

The investigation exposed the gruesome method used to dispose of the dogs. The animals are taken into the forest and hung from trees so that they are slowly strangled or starve to death

*1 Slaughtered in 1995 in the U.S. were: 7.5 billion chickens, 281 million turkeys, 96.5 million hogs, and 1.5 million veal calves, more than 99% of whom never see the outdoors except through slats in the sides of the truck that takes them to their doom. The annual toll also includes 35.8 million cattle and 4.6 million sheep and lambs. Increasing numbers of dairy cattle and so-called "milk fed spring lamb,"raised in the equivalent of veal crates, also never go outside. (The total number of chickens slaughtered each year probably exceeds 9 billion; in addition to the 7.5 cited above 1.5 billion more are spent laying hens, slaughtered for animal feed rather than for hu-

man consumption.)

*13 For more than a quarter of a century this scientist at the University of Chicago, deprived animals of sleep. He started out keeping rats awake for up to 24 hours and then letting them recover.

He moved on to total sleep deprivation: he kept rats awake until their bodies could no longer cope and they died of exhaustion. This took anywhere from 11 to 32 days. To prepare the helpless animals for this long nightmarish journey to death, the vivisector stuck electrodes in their skulls, sewed wires to their hearts, and surgically buried thermometers in their stomachs, so that he could track their temperatures and brain waves. To make blood drawing easier (for him), he snaked catheters through their jugular veins, down their necks, and into their hearts.

Once the rats were wired up like circuit boards, he placed them on disks suspended above water. When the rats started to enter the forbidden sleep stage, the disks automatically rotated. If the rats didn't get up and walk back and forth across the tilting disk that was their "home," they were dumped into the water. Eventually, after their fur turned oily and yellowish brown and fell out in clumps, they developed ulcers on their feet and tails, their body fat dissolved, and the rats died. So what did the scientist hope to discover? In his own words, "We established that rats die after 17 days of total sleep deprivation. Thus, at least for the rat, sleep is essential."

*8 Who would do this? By day he was a successful commodities trader. By night he went home to his luxury condominium and tortured his cat. One night he nailed Ginger's front paw to a board so she couldn't reach the bowl of food just inches away. And even had she been able to, she couldn't have swallowed because of-the scars in her mouth caused by the acid cocktail her sadistic master had thrown in her face a few nights earlier. Now Ginger was starving to death.

Like so many abusers, when things got really bad, this sadist would take his "injured" cat to a veterinary hospital for treatment, but when he got her back, the abuse would start again. Three times he brought Ginger to the same private Manhattan hospital. Finally, suspecting that there was more to these injuries, the staff called in the ASPCA Humane Law Enforcement Division to investigate. When their investigating officer saw Ginger's serious condition, they rushed her to the ASPCA's Bergh Memorial Hospital for emergency treatment. Ginger's owner finally admitted that she was abused. It took three months of treatment and surgery to produce a viable Ginger. When Roger A. Caras heard of Ginger's story he adopted her and brought her home to his farm.

*4 "Humane slaughter," wrote Professor Gary L. Fancione, "is an oxymoron." The extant federal and state legislation cannot remove the terror of animals who are transported long distances, sold at unlicensed auction, driven in situations that cause panic and injury and held in packing houses where the smell and sound of death are overwhelming before an animal itself is slaughtered.

"The inhumanity of slaughter will never end while there is a market for the meat the packers produce. It is merely the brutal end of a lifetime of suffering." (And, we must add: There will be a "market for the meat" as long as animals are perceived as mere *things* to be owned, sold, slaughtered and, eaten.)

*1 "More than two million dogs and cats are killed each year

The Need to Know

for use in the international fur trade," The Humane Society of the United States announced in a press release, in February, 1999. An 18-month investigation by a nine-person team led by the HSUS Vice-president of Investigative Services Rick Swain and German journalist Manfred Karreman found that dogs and cats are cruelly slaughtered for the manufacture of fur clothing and accessories worldwide. Dog and cat fur is sold in the U.S. as hats, gloves, decorative accessories, and even toy stuffed animals. The HSUS investigation focused on practices in China, Thailand, and the Philippines. The release described live dogs being kept in an unheated room in bitter cold, surrounded by the bodies of dead dogs hanging from hooks at a dog farm in Harbin China. Undercover video footage documented "animals dying slowly by suffocation, hanging, bludgeoning or bleeding to death."

*12 The killing of more than five million "purpose-bred laboratory animals in the United Kingdom has been documented by animal rights groups as well as Government officials and laboratory scientists. But these animals weren't used in experiments. These animals were "surplus"-brought into this world and killed because they were "unneeded." The species documented include, but are not limited to mice, rats, monkeys, dogs, cats, and rabbits.

The Ministry of Defense (MOD) reasoned their killing of three times more animals than they used "because they were not suitable" for their tests. The MOD added, however, that this level of surplus killing is consistent with normal practice.

Reasons given from the home office for such a large number of animals being bred and killed was the inability to predict actual supply and demand, as well as specifics desired in research such as age, weight, and sex. Methods of killing include gassing, lethal injection, and neck breaking.

While there is no available study of surplus killing in the United States, one can assume a similar code of practice exists. Given that the U.S. uses at least 10 times more animals in research than the United Kingdom, the number of "extra" animals is assuredly far greater.

*14 What do you do with 440 Chinese squirrels shipped illegally without the proper papers? They could introduce a non native disease. Shoot them? drown them? wring their necks? or electrocute them?

It was in Amsterdam that KLM Royal Dutch Airlines was confronted with this what do you do question, and they had an answer. Shred them alive in a chicken shredder, yes shred them! And because they are KLM Royal Dutch Airlines they apologized for their "unethical" conduct.

14

Closing Comments

Unlike the word animal, which pertains to a class of
sentient beings with which we are familiar, the word tyrannize tends to occasionally evoke questions. The story of ghoul-
ish conduct outlined in the previous section, which is a micro
-catalogue of ongoing tyrannous human behavior, should, I
believe, be an answer.

But it bears repeating: We will never know the whole
story of human-generated tyranny suffered by animals. But
we should know why so many areas of Partisan concern, such
as the "culling" of deer, or the bumpkin pigeon shoots, as
well as a myriad of other revolting examples of human tyranny, were not mentioned on these pages. The reader might
perceive this as a serious omission, and the reason for the
omission must be explained.

The overriding principle that rebuffs every partisan
prejudicial argument and should define any act obviously
harmful to animals as unacceptable human conduct subject
to punishment as prescribed by law, derives from John Locke's
thesis, and constitutes an animal's right to be free of human
tyranny.

Closing Comments

The proposition, "every man has a property in his own person; this nobody has a right to but himself," unlike an axiom was not self-evident to many people, and was apparently, and to a marked degree in defiance of popular opinion, but was initially capable, as it is now, of being validly supported by reason.

The deduced overarching principle supported by reason is that: every sentient being has, in human terms of reference, an inviolable property in itself by virtue of the veneration of property rights which should, if we are to abide by our own principle of justice, prohibit ownership and brutal exploitation of animals, as it does by and large, of humans. Thus, every form of tyrannous practice (with the exception of subsistence exploitation by indigenous people as described above) should be prohibited and not again be allowed to knowingly exist. From which it follows that neither the deer, nor the pigeons, nor any other animal should be fair game for routine or random tyranny. On the other hand, as mentioned above, violent reaction to an extraordinary life-threatening situation such as a mad dog posing an immanent danger to the life of people or other animals would not be defined as an instance of tyranous practice

The totality of effects of an equitable new world for animals, both domesticated and wild, would be of great positive and negative magnitude. Positive, inasmuch as the habit of human-generated suffering and violent death for billions upon billions of animals would cease to be the norm. Positive, because justice would be extended and prevail as never before in the history of Mr. Homo Sapiens. Negative, in terms of economic and psychological dislocations in the human community.

Dislocations would be painful, though temporary, and rarely, if ever, fatal. We are not referring to anything like the

Closing Comments

aftermath of a catastrophe such as an earthquake, that occurs with little or no warning, with its ensuing destruction and death. We are here referring to dislocations that will have paradoxically resulted from a new dispensation of justice, centuries in the making, for the animal kingdom.

It is idle to believe that a partisan majority will relinquish its brutal dominion of animals without a drawn-out Partisan versus partisan conflict. It will continue to be, loosely speaking, a bloodless equivalent of conventional war, fought with words written and spoken, and orderly demonstrations, the conflicting objectives being to outlaw the tyrannizing of animals on the one hand, and to maintain the status quo, a slaughterhouse ethos, on the other hand.

And Partisans I believe, will prevail, because of our ever-increasing ability to transmit information such as the unceasing **preventable** evils suffered by animals. It's not a stand-still world, it's a world of perpetual change from which it follows that it's possible if not probable, that institutionalized as well as a surfeit of other human-generated tyrannies affecting animals will be: *given sufficient Partisan power and determination,* relegated to the limbo of abominable habits and customs.

That there will be many questions, and much criticism evoked by a book so critical of the "dominion of the herd," which left so much unsaid, is not only expected but welcome. Was it not inconsistent to suggest exemption for indigenous people from sanctions for tyrannizing animals? Can we realistically expect the termination of vivisection: a procedure that allegedly might lead to "cures" for various intractable diseases?

There can be no denying the fact that native people tyrannize animals to obtain subsistence nourishment. And there can be no denying the truth that in an inhospitable en-

Closing Comments

vironment, where hunger is a possibility, starvation and death is not an attractive alternative to a hunting and fishing ethos. Meat, fowl, and a preponderance of fish is their primary source of nutrition, and food brought in, is, for many Eskimos, not affordable. Such circumstances seem to justify exemption for a protracted period from sanctions for tyrannizing animals. Perhaps such exemption would provide an adequate amount of preparatory time for the transition away from the hunting ethos and, would preclude the tyrannizing of humans, to prevent their tyrannizing of animals.

But how, one might ask, can we reconcile such exemption with the precept that animals shall not be tyrannized by humans? The answer lies in perception of the limitations imposed by realities, and a realistic perspective. It's certainly not morally acceptable, even if it were lawfully possible, to order thousands of people who know no other way of life, to immediately stop tyrannizing animals, pack their bags, and leave for warmer climes. A realistic perspective lies in again perceiving the truth of a variation of the words as cited above, i.e., beyond one's power to act humanely, one is not obliged to act, relative to the predatoriness of indigenous people in a harsh hostile environment (as well as to wild animals living in the natural state). Failure to immediately universalize a moral ethic does not diminish its regional or national value.

The seemingly irresoluble vivisection question may be one of the oldest nonstop polemics on the planet. The arguments which keep happening as if they had never happened before are, briefly stated, the alleged benefits to mankind and animals, versus the price, in terms of suffering and death for animals, tangible and intangible harm to people including death, and expenditures of vast sums of money.

Plato had it right when he observed that what was given to the eyes is the intention of the soul, and indeed it is. We

Closing Comments

perceive selectively and fail to see all of the relevant factors, and we are all, at times, guilty as charged. Such was the offense of the National Academy of Sciences Institute of Medicine's hurrah for vivisection, in the August, 1991 issue of *Consumers Research*. Their message: Many of us are here because of the continuity of life imparted by the control of disease through animal research. And many of the benefits that accrue to animals would not exist were it not gleaned from animal research.

These myopic observations were made for the sole purpose of justifying vivisection, and are based on three assumptions: 1) The control of disease can only be achieved by vivisection as practiced. 2) An activity of international scope such as vivisection, affecting both man and animals adversely and favorably, can be correctly labeled as an unequivocal good to justify its existence and perpetuation. 3) People have a moral right (because they still have a legal right) to tyrannize animals in the pursuit of knowledge.

As we have seen, there have been and are successful methods to combat disease sans vivisection. Is it not reasonable to say that given our habitual economic and academic opportunism, and tendency to pursue the path of least resistance, the quest for humane alternatives was a victim of indifference and neglect?

The contention that "many of us are here because we did not die as children," thanks to vivisection, is an instance of suppressing intangible, but relevant evidence by selecting only that which is in support of an idea. Suppressed is the fact (perhaps unconsciously) that "many of us are here" must also include the many that were here such as Hitler, Stalin, Pol Pot, and the many tyrants that are still here in the 90s, and responsible for unconscionable pillage, rape, and murder. We can know only in principle how many tens of millions of

Closing Comments

people were mortally victimized, and to what extent vivisection was a proximal link in the causal chain of relevant factors that are not given to the eyes of those who do not wish see and, those who wish to see. The attempt to justify the practice of vivisection on the basis of an apparently truncated account of reality is misleadingly incomplete because it entails a non-exhaustive classification that does not include obscure but germane realities. The only thing that argument can prove is the desire to perpetuate barbarism. "But" it will be rejoined, "do you think the search for cures for AIDS, cancer, and other dreadful things should come to a halt because of fear of a hypothetical Hitler et al in the future? Or do you think that research in the past should not have occurred because the lives saved could include those of aggressive monsters?"

These are questions which only a disgruntled misanthrope could answer in the affirmative. It is not research that should be called to a halt, or should not have happened, but the infliction of cruelty and death upon helpless animals euphemistically labeled "research" by tyrannous power. To characterize such "research" as an unqualified good is misleadingly deceptive. And to say that "we need to search for medical knowledge" is true, but redundant, unless we stipulate, "but not by tyrannizing animals."

To this condition, resolute partisans will object, and to what they will be objecting must be made clear. Objection would be to the testimony of empirical truth, definitional truth, and logical validity. From the premise x is an animal subject to human property rights it is inferred that therefore, x shall be exploited in the interest of humans in whatever way deemed advantageous or necessary. It should now be clear that this argument is based on a the same legal fiction used to rationalize slavery.

Closing Comments

The partisan world notwithstanding, it seems that we can realistically expect the termination of vivisection in the foreseeable future, for two reasons. 1)The condonation of that practice is in violation of an unambiguous and well-nigh universal standard of justice as described above in section three. 2) We may soon expect a scientific breakthrough with an alleged potential to build objects, whether it be common bricks, or a human heart from the building blocks of atoms and molecules. Theoretically we could dispense with animals and manufacture steaks from grass (as cows do) and tiny instruments (machines) could be employed within an organism to repair ailing parts such as cells. Ageing could allegedly be significantly delayed or arrested.

The concept of nano-technology was conceived by Nobel laureate Richard Feynman and first votarist to earn a doctorate in the field was K. Erick Drexler. The following excerpts are from a Foresight Institute Briefing Paper #3, written by John Walker.

Over thirty years ago Richard Feynman pointed out that physicists knew no limits to prevent us from doing engineering at the level of atoms. His words are as true today as the day he spoke them.

"So what we're talking about is making the next big jump to building systems a thousand times smaller than the ones we're making today; to go all the way to the bottom and start working with individual atoms.

"This is called molecular engineering, or nano-technology. Eric Drexler defines this as control of the structure of matter at the molecular level.

"Precise atomic level fabrication has previously been done only by living biological organisms. We are entering an era when some of the barriers between engineered and living systems will begin to fall. Biology builds its structures from

Closing Comments

the bottom up, at the molecular level, and in three dimensions. Engineers are learning how to do this. The remarkable thing about molecular engineering is that it looks like there are many different ways to get there and, at the moment, rapid progress is being made along every path-all at the same time.

"In 1988, a group at Du Pont led by William DeGrado designed a new protein called alpha-4 from scratch, and manufactured it in their laboratory. This protein, which never existed in nature, is more stable than natural proteins its size. Researchers around the world are now looking at proteins as molecular structures they can design and build, just as an IC designer lays out a chip.

"And so, we can begin to see the outlines of the sixth industrial revolution: moving from micrometer scale devices to nano-meter scale devices. Current progress suggests the revolution may happen within this decade, perhaps starting within five years. What can we make with it? Well, anything we can design and model that's built with atoms. Think about that.

"In fact, if we want to make objects on the meter scale with molecular engineering, we're going to have to design replicating machines. The vacuum tube I showed you has about 10^{23} atoms in it, and if you try to build something that large atom by atom, it's going to take pretty long. If you add an atom every second, it'll take 10^{23} seconds, which is a real problem because that's a million times longer than the current age of the universe. But, if you can get your molecular machine to crank out copies of themselves, you can set up a chain reaction that can generate numbers on that scale quite rapidly. That's how biology manufactures bacteria, butterflies, and buffalos, and it works very well.

"But the real question I haven't answered yet is this. Is it actually possible to make these little machines out of at-

Closing Comments

oms and then get them to replicate themselves, or is this all just a pile of hooey, as ridiculous as, say, putting 16 million transistors on a piece of silicon the size of your finger nail? "Let's look at how we might design such a machine. Here's a little gadget that looks like a lunar lander, but considerably smaller. It stands about 225 nano-meters high. This device is designed to operate within a living system, to seek out cells of a particular type, land on them by extending its legs, then inject them with material stored in the tank at the top. You could design something like this, for example, to locate cancerous cells in a human body and kill them. "Could something like this be built? Could it possibly work? Yes. Whether or not it will work remains to be seen. The fact that America, Europe, and Japan are spending a total of over $300 million on nano-technology research should serve to take the edge off skepticism. Pertinent information can be found at the WTEC webpage, http://itri.loyola. edu/nano/welcome.htm."

Another germane factor that must be acknowledged is the science of molecular medicine, which purportedly holds great promise for the conquest of disease. Can we believe that the triad of molecular medicine, nano-technology, and the plea of necessity, will not be if not disallowed, the new rationale for brutalizing animals in the future?

Holding a brief for animals, I could not fail to include the above informative data, which could portend unprecedented change, including, as things now stand, an increase in the suffering of animals. In the absence of significant *Partisan induced attitudinal and moral change,* we can be quite certain that before nano-devices are used to repair tissue in human bodies, they would be tested in the bodies of animals. That possibility, in addition to extant realities makes the need of humane attitudinal and moral change a matter of incalculable importance. It seems possible, given the unquali-

Closing Comments

fied success of nano-technology, that molecular-engineered machines will one day revolutionize medical research and medicine to a degree that this Partisan can't imagine. But possibilities of what may be must not be allowed to obscure extant realities and the crucial need for Partisan-induced change.

In the last year of the twentieth century as at all previous times, and possibly, if not probably, till the end of time, mortals, whether human or nonhuman will suffer afflictions that will resist attempts at alleviation and cure. On that ground we can predict that the quest for knowledge to alleviate and cure will probably continue to be the task of science. But it is not the province of science, politicians, or publics to obtrude upon the realm of legal or moral rights, whether of human or nonhuman animals. Therefore, given objectives which must be realized without tyrannizing human or nonhuman animals, it is the task of science to discover nonviolent means.

As we know from our inveiglement with slavery, defining the slave as property tacitly implied the legal right to exploit or brutalize the slave, for which there never was a moral right. If just one "master's" brutal act was unacceptable conduct, with what word or words of condemnation shall we deprecate the goings-on manifest in section Thirteen.

Most of the heartlessness responsible for the brutality described in section thirteen is that of an inhumane minority within a predominantly omnivorous society.

The majority on the other hand, which is not to be equated with the "inhumane minority," is responsible, however unconsciously, for infinitely more harming, suffering, and violent death of animals than the minority. That blameworthy fact can be attributed to an omnivorous lifestyle that creates a demand for the flesh of animals in our Potemkin world,

Closing Comments

ostensibly committed to the right, the good, and the just. A world well insulated by indifference to, or ignorance of the realities of a plethora of legal atrocities including, but not limited to factory farms, abattoirs, vivisection laboratories, and fur farms. Thus the flesh mongers, furriers, drug cartels, and collateral industries prosper while clergymen hold forth on the "Golden Rule," apparently unmindful or unconcerned that their homily is absurdly unfitting in a world or society that brutally exploits and kills billions upon billions of animals annually.

We can speculate, but we can't know what the future holds in store for the Animal Kingdom, but we know that "change is an ever-lasting reality." We should know that neither animals, broadly defined nor people should be morally, logically, or legally classified as mere property. But animals are classified as mere property, and brutally victimized in conformity with "the tyrants plea" in the alleged private and collective interest of their human owners. The necessary condition of an unprecedented change is an overwhelming power of will to reject with condemnation the animals as property hellishness.

Such change will not just happen, but must be made to happen through incremental steps. And by whom if not Partisans who strive for and foresee a world in which the planned and methodical or wanton brutalizing and killing of animals in any context by humans, will be classified as unlawful criminal behavior, and not knowingly tolerated.

Sources of the Need to Know

*1   Animal People
*2   The Gorilla Foundation
*3   International Fund for Animal Welfare
*4   The Animals Voice *
*5   Physicians Committee for Responsible Medicine
*6   Doris Day Animal League
*7   Farm Sanctuary
*8   American Society for the Prevention of Cruelty
     to Animals
*9   American Horse Protective Association
*10 International Society for Animal Rights
*11 International Wildlife Coalition
*12 American Antivivisection Society
*13 People for the Ethical Treatment of Animals
*14 Chicago Tribune
*15 In Defense of Animals
*16 Animal Legal Defense Fund
*17 Performing Animals Welfare Society
*18 Animal Protection Institute
*19 World Society for Protection of Animals
*20 Illinois Animal Action

*   The Animals Voice has merged with the Animal
     Agenda

Index

Index

Index

Korea, 123-124
Kosher slaughter, 121

Laurdes Garza-Ocans, 60
Lincoln, Abraham, 48
Loeb, Jerod, M., 51
Locke, John, 12-15
Law of Contradiction, 17
LD50, 61
Livestock auction, 98-99
Letterman Army Institute, 96-127
Lincoln Park Zoo, 112
Lobsters, 134

Madison, James, 12
Madras Corporation, 124
Malaria, 20
Manatee, 100
Measles, 49
Merino sheep, 80
Mexico, 94
Military experiments, 89
Misanthrope, 34
Monkey, 96
Moral necessity, 22
Morrison, Adrian, 100
Moses, 31
MRC-5 Cells, 60
Mt. Everest, 64
Mulesing, 81
Muslin, Halal Slaughter, 121

National Research Council, 19
Necessity, 37-45
Nebraska, 102
New England Journal of
    Medicine, 103
New Mexico, 105
Nilson, Greta, 64

Novic, J.P., 96
Nylon parka, 64

Officer Plennick, 37
Omak suicide race, 107-108
Ontario Canada, 116
Open Heart surgery, 49
Orangutan, 117

Pancretic transplants, 5
Partisan justice, 7
Pascal Blaise, 6
Paul of Tarsus, 31
Pharmagene Laboratories, 60-61
Philippines, 124
Pierre, Kaitia Jean, 107
Peta, 104-118
Pigs, 93-104
Poliomyelitis, 23-24-25-49
Pollution, 65
Premarin, 109-110
Primordial life, 14
Prince Edward Island, 131
Property, 17-18
Proprietas, 13
Proprius, 13
Physicians Committee for Respon-
    sible Medicine, 20
Physical laws of motion, 21
Puangham, Preech, 113
Puerto Rico, 118
Puppy Mills, 93-128

Rabbit, 35-108
Rabies, 49
Race horse, 92-107
Rat, 54
Reader's Digest, 49
Realism, 11

Index

✍ Notes ✍

✍ Notes ✍

✍ Notes ✍

✍ Notes ✍

✍ Notes ✍

✍ Notes ✍